CW01246283

# Studies on Entrepreneurship, Structural Change and Industrial Dynamics

**Series editors**
João Leitão
University of Beira Interior, Covilhã, Portugal

Tessaleno Devezas
University of Beira Interior, Covilhã, Portugal

The 'Studies on Entrepreneurship, Structural Change and Industrial Dynamics' series showcases exceptional scholarly work being developed on the still unexplored complex relationship between entrepreneurship, structural change and industrial dynamics, by addressing structural and technological determinants of the evolutionary pathway of innovative and entrepreneurial activity.

The series invites proposals based on sound research methodologies and approaches to the above topics. Volumes in the series may include research monographs and edited/contributed works.

More information about this series at http://www.springer.com/series/15330

Vanessa Ratten
Editor

# Technological Progress, Inequality and Entrepreneurship

From Consumer Division to Human Centricity

☒ Springer

*Editor*
Vanessa Ratten
Department of Entrepreneurship,
Innovation and Marketing
La Trobe Business School
Melbourne, VIC, Australia

ISSN 2511-2023 ISSN 2511-2031 (electronic)
Studies on Entrepreneurship, Structural Change and Industrial Dynamics
ISBN 978-3-030-26244-0 ISBN 978-3-030-26245-7 (eBook)
https://doi.org/10.1007/978-3-030-26245-7

© Springer Nature Switzerland AG 2020
This work is subject to copyright. All rights are reserved by the Publisher, whether the whole or part of the material is concerned, specifically the rights of translation, reprinting, reuse of illustrations, recitation, broadcasting, reproduction on microfilms or in any other physical way, and transmission or information storage and retrieval, electronic adaptation, computer software, or by similar or dissimilar methodology now known or hereafter developed.
The use of general descriptive names, registered names, trademarks, service marks, etc. in this publication does not imply, even in the absence of a specific statement, that such names are exempt from the relevant protective laws and regulations and therefore free for general use.
The publisher, the authors, and the editors are safe to assume that the advice and information in this book are believed to be true and accurate at the date of publication. Neither the publisher nor the authors or the editors give a warranty, express or implied, with respect to the material contained herein or for any errors or omissions that may have been made. The publisher remains neutral with regard to jurisdictional claims in published maps and institutional affiliations.

This Springer imprint is published by the registered company Springer Nature Switzerland AG.
The registered company address is: Gewerbestrasse 11, 6330 Cham, Switzerland

# Acknowledgments

Firstly, I would like to thank Dr Prashanth Mahagaonkar for his expertise and guidance with this book. Secondly, I thank the authors of the chapters. It takes a lot of time and effort to come up with an idea for a book and then obtain quality contributors. So I am grateful to the authors of these chapters for their hard work and dedication. In editing this book, I have thought a lot about the way technology is progressing in terms of artificial intelligence and the use of robots. As a teacher and researcher of technology innovation, I find the pace of innovation interesting particularly with regard to mobile communication. Thirdly, I dedicate this book on technological progress, inequality, and entrepreneurship to my mum, Kaye Ratten. My mum was an entrepreneur and had an ability to predict future technology trends. Many years ago, it was my mum who told me to buy Google shares but unfortunately instead of investing in them I watched in awe at the increase in share price but also resulting technological innovations including Gmail, Google Pay, and other services. In my mum's lifetime, there was a big change in the use of technology including transitioning from typewriters to computers. When I first started at university, I used a typewriter for some of my assignments but quickly changed to a computer because of its ease of use. At the same time in 1995 during my first year at university, email was just introduced. We now take for granted email and use it on a daily basis, but thinking back to the 1990s it is amazing to see how far technology has progressed. Fast forward to 2019 when I am editing this book, I can think about how much technology has progressed. This includes the lightweight laptop computer I am using and mobile phone to access electronic information. This progression in technology has resulted in a shift toward entrepreneurs and entrepreneurship. I hope the chapters in this book spur more interest in technological progress, inequality, and entrepreneurship.

# Contents

**Technological Progress, Inequality and Entrepreneurship: From Consumer Division to Human Centricity** .................... 1
Vanessa Ratten

**Transformative Changes and Developments of the Coworking Model: A Narrative Review** ........................................ 9
Marko Orel and Ondřej Dvouletý

**The Role of ICT in Involving the Tourist and in Sustainability of Tourism Destinations** .................................... 29
Célia M. Q. Ramos, Georgette Andraz, and Irene Cardoso

**Technology-Based Tourism Businesses: Extracting Actionable Knowledge and Insights from Social Networks** .................. 47
Jose Ramón-Saura, Pedro R. Palos-Sanchez, and María de la Cruz del Río-Rama

**Digital Accessibility on Institutional Websites of Portuguese Tourism** ... 67
Fátima Matos Silva and Isabel Borges

**The Ethical Assumptions in Higher Education** .................. 87
Rui Pedro Lopes, Cristina Mesquita, Amador Durán-Sánchez, and Juan R. Coca

**Geotourism in Latin America and Caribbean UNESCO Global Geoparks: Contribution for Sustainable Development Goals** ......... 107
Emmaline M. Rosado-González, José Luis Palacio-Prieto, and Artur Abreu Sá

**Social Innovation in Refugee Support: Investigating Prerequisites Towards a Conceptual Framework** ............................ 123
Phyllis McNally, Nikolaos Apostolopoulos, and Haya Al-Dajani

# List of Contributors

**Haya Al-Dajani**  Plymouth University, Plymouth, UK

**Georgette Andraz**  ESGHT & CEFAGE, Universidade do Algarve, Faro, Portugal

**Nikolaos Apostolopoulos**  Plymouth University, Plymouth, UK

**Isabel Borges**  Department of Tourism, Heritage and Culture, Universidade Portucalense Infante D. Henrique, Porto, Portugal
REMIT – Research on Economics, Management and Information Technologies, Portucalense University, Porto, Portugal
CEGOT – Centre of Studies on Geography and Spatial Planning, University of Coimbra, Coimbra, Portugal
CEPESE – Centre for Studies of Population, Economy and Society, Porto, Portugal

**Irene Cardoso**  ISEG, Lisbon, Portugal

**Juan R. Coca**  Faculty of Education of Soria, Department of Sociology and Social Work, University of Valladolid, Soria, Spain

**María de la Cruz del Río-Rama**  Department of Business Organization and Marketing, University of Vigo, Pontevedra, Spain

**Amador Durán-Sánchez**  Faculty of Business, Finance and Tourism, Department of Financial Economics and Accounting, University of Extremadura, Caceres, Spain

**Ondřej Dvouletý**  Department of Entrepreneurship, Faculty of Business Administration, University of Economics in Prague, Prague, Czech Republic

**Rui Pedro Lopes**  Research Center on Digitalization and Intelligent Robotics, Instituto Politécnico de Bragança, Bragança, Portugal

**Phyllis McNally**  Plymouth University, Plymouth, UK

**Cristina Mesquita**  Research Center on Basic Education, Instituto Politécnico de Bragança, Bragança, Portugal

**Marko Orel** Department of Entrepreneurship, Faculty of Business Administration, University of Economics in Prague, Prague, Czech Republic

**José Luis Palacio-Prieto** Earth Sciences National School and Geography Institute, National Autonomous University of Mexico, Mexico City, Mexico

**Pedro R. Palos-Sanchez** Department of Business Administration and Marketing, University of Sevilla, Sevilla, Spain

**Célia M. Q. Ramos** ESGHT, CIEO & CEFAGE, Universidade do Algarve, Faro, Portugal

**Vanessa Ratten** Department of Entrepreneurship, Innovation and Marketing, La Trobe Business School, Melbourne, VIC, Australia

**Emmaline M. Rosado-González** UNESCO Chair on Geoparks, Sustainable Regional Development and Healthy Lifestyles, University of Trás-os-Montes e Alto Douro, Vila Real, Portugal
Geoscience Centre of University of Coimbra, Coimbra, Portugal

**Artur Abreu Sá** UNESCO Chair on Geoparks, Sustainable Regional Development and Healthy Lifestyles, University of Trás-os-Montes e Alto Douro, Vila Real, Portugal
Geoscience Centre of University of Coimbra, Coimbra, Portugal

**Jose Ramón-Saura** Department of Business Economics, Rey Juan Carlos University, Madrid, Spain

**Fátima Matos Silva** Department of Tourism, Heritage and Culture, Universidade Portucalense Infante D. Henrique, Porto, Portugal
REMIT – Research on Economics, Management and Information Technologies, Portucalense University, Porto, Portugal
Faculdade de Letras da Universidade do Porto-FLUP, CITCEM – Centre for Transdisciplinary Research Culture, Space and Memory, Research Centre (uID 04059), Oporto University, Porto, Portugal

# List of Figures

**The Role of ICT in Involving the Tourist and in Sustainability of Tourism Destinations**

| | | |
|---|---|---|
| Fig. 1 | Functions of the tourism destination. Source: Adapted from Giménez (2006: 16–22) | 32 |
| Fig. 2 | Relation between the travel phases and the use of ICT. Source: Adapted from Gretzel et al. (2006) | 33 |
| Fig. 3 | Conceptual model of the destination tourism product. Source: Adapted from Murphy et al. (2000: 46) | 35 |
| Fig. 4 | Conceptual model of the destination tourism product. Source: Adapted from Buhalis and Amaranggana (2015) | 36 |

**Technology-Based Tourism Businesses: Extracting Actionable Knowledge and Insights from Social Networks**

| | | |
|---|---|---|
| Fig. 1 | Main types of analysis in social media analytics. Source: The authors | 53 |
| Fig. 2 | Main UGC topics for digital tourism on Twitter. Source: The authors | 55 |

**Digital Accessibility on Institutional Websites of Portuguese Tourism**

| | | |
|---|---|---|
| Fig. 1 | *AcessMonitor* indexes of the websites analysed. Source: Author's own figure | 78 |
| Fig. 2 | Percentage of level A errors presented in the websites analysed. Source: Author's own figure | 79 |

**The Ethical Assumptions in Higher Education**

| | | |
|---|---|---|
| Fig. 1 | Development of ethical skills. Source: Author's own figure | 102 |

**Geotourism in Latin America and Caribbean UNESCO Global Geoparks: Contribution for Sustainable Development Goals**

| | | |
|---|---|---|
| Fig. 1 | Contribution of the four LAC UGGps to the targets chosen from SDG 8. Source: Author's own figure | 118 |
| Fig. 2 | Contribution of the four LAC UGGps to the targets chosen from SDG 10. Source: Author's own figure | 119 |
| Fig. 3 | Contribution of the four LAC UGGps to the targets chosen from SDG 15. Source: Author's own figure | 119 |

**Social Innovation in Refugee Support: Investigating Prerequisites Towards a Conceptual Framework**

| | | |
|---|---|---|
| Fig. 1 | Analytical themes | 131 |
| Fig. 2 | Stakeholder involvement (Source: Phyllis McNally, 2018) | 134 |

# List of Tables

**The Role of ICT in Involving the Tourist and in Sustainability of Tourism Destinations**

| | | |
|---|---|---|
| Table 1 | The use of ICT for searching information about tourist destination | 40 |
| Table 2 | Reliability of information online | 40 |
| Table 3 | Reliability of information and education level | 41 |
| Table 4 | Reliability of information and education level as grouping variable (Kruskal Wallis Test results) | 41 |
| Table 5 | Importance of sharing information through social networks | 41 |
| Table 6 | Influence do the travel comments shared on the internet | 42 |
| Table 7 | Relevance of mobile devices during the trip | 42 |
| Table 8 | Main action using ICT during the trip | 43 |
| Table 9 | Social network most used to share trip information | 43 |

**Technology-Based Tourism Businesses: Extracting Actionable Knowledge and Insights from Social Networks**

| | | |
|---|---|---|
| Table 1 | Previous research on technological based tourism businesses | 50 |
| Table 2 | Research on UGC in tourism | 51 |
| Table 3 | Summary of technologies and business model for digital tourism | 61 |

**Digital Accessibility on Institutional Websites of Portuguese Tourism**

| | | |
|---|---|---|
| Table 1 | Characterization of some elements of the websites analysed | 82 |

**The Ethical Assumptions in Higher Education**

| | | |
|---|---|---|
| Table 1 | Collected data | 92 |

**Geotourism in Latin America and Caribbean UNESCO Global Geoparks: Contribution for Sustainable Development Goals**

Table 1 Targets selected for each SDG ..................................... 117

**Social Innovation in Refugee Support: Investigating Prerequisites Towards a Conceptual Framework**

Table 1 Analytical themes, categories and examples of raw data ............ 132

# Technological Progress, Inequality and Entrepreneurship: From Consumer Division to Human Centricity

**Vanessa Ratten**

**Abstract** During the past decade changes made as a result of technological innovation have been profound and impacted society. The aim of this chapter is to examine the inequality and entrepreneurship that has resulted from this technological progress in order to understand better how to manage the change. This is important as there has been a growing inequality gap in society in terms of access to emerging technology that needs the help of entrepreneurs and policy planners to readdress. The role of consumers in this change is discussed as a way of progressing the literature on technological innovation and entrepreneurship. Practical and theoretical implications from technological progress in terms of human centricity are stated.

**Keywords** Entrepreneurship · Inequality · Technological progress

## 1 Introduction

There has been considerable technological advances in the past decade that have transformed the way people live and behave (Ratten, Ferreira, & Fernandes, 2017). This has created societal change but also led to inequality amongst the rich and poor in terms of access to services. Inequality is a rising area of interest in entrepreneurship studies that will gain academic interest due to an increasing amount of focus on technology innovation (Tajeddini, Altinay, & Ratten, 2017). There is a range of technology devices from phones and wearables that need to be analysed as a way of providing guidance on how to address inequality challenges in society. We are now living in a technology-based society and new technology will further intensify the importance of technology to everyday activity.

---

V. Ratten (✉)
Department of Entrepreneurship, Innovation and Marketing, La Trobe Business School, Melbourne, VIC, Australia
e-mail: v.ratten@latrobe.edu.au

Technological progress is a widely used concept that is frequently discussed in the media but seldom specifically discussed in terms of inequality. Rapid advancements in technology have changed the way people conduct their daily lives but at the same time made people reliant on technology (Ratten, 2015). This is due to technology being embedded in society and governments using it as a way to interact with citizens. As technology has progressed there has been plenty of debate about privacy and ethical concerns. This is due to a need to use technology without there being other alternatives. More electronic information is transmitted and stored but this has raised questions regarding privacy concerns.

There are two main approaches to understanding technological progress: consumer division and human centricity. In the past, technology advanced without the help of consumers, but this has changed with more communication between users and developers becoming evident. Open innovation and the sharing economy have further pushed consumers into disseminating their ideas with companies in a way that was never considered in the past (Ratten & Tajeddini, 2017). The idea of co-creation and collaboration has become more important due to issues like social responsibility and sustainability being popular. For this reason, it is crucial to make humans central to the ideation process and enable greater sharing of ideas. This will help encourage entrepreneurship but also enable social forms of innovation that address inequality to emerge (Ferreira, Ratten, & Dana, 2017).

The research on technological progress is impeded due to the fragmented theoretical frameworks used to describe the phenomena. There are numerous theories that can be used to understand technology progress that depend on the disciplinary background of the researcher. For those coming from an engineering or mathematical background, there is a need for more formulastic and hypothesis testing regarding technological innovation. Social science researchers on the other hand tend to use more behavioural theories to understand technological innovation. This can result in oversimplifying complex relationships due to the focus on human-computer interaction. Thus, researchers will interpret results differently depending on their theoretical framework. A new theory that recognises the inequality in society from technological progress is required. This will serve to incorporate other theories but tie together the findings. In addition, multiple levels of analysis from the individual, community, business and region are needed to understand the effects of technological progress (Ferreira & Ratten, 2017). This will lead to better interpretations about technological progress and more clearer results. Utilising different levels of analysis will enable a pluralistic view of technological innovation to emerge. Although care must be taken to identify the technology innovation and respect different conceptualisations of the topic. In this way, more cumulative knowledge can be acquired about the role of inequality and its impact on entrepreneurship (Ferreira, Fernandes, & Ratten, 2015).

## 2 Entrepreneurship and Technology Progress

Entrepreneurship is a product of technological progress and involves the use of creative thinking in business ventures. There are different forms of entrepreneurship stemming from technological progress including international, social and sustainable but all involve some kind of creative change (Jones, Jones, Williams-Burnett, & Ratten, 2017). As Parente, El Tarabishy, Vesci, and Botti (2018: 30) states "there is now a rising awareness of the potential impact that entrepreneurial behaviours have, good and bad, not only on economic development, but also on many other aspects of individual and societal life". Thus, it is important to analyse the positive and negatives from technological progress in order to better understand how society is progressing (Ratten, 2016). The impact of information and communication technology is amplified when individuals need it for their lifestyle. This has meant mobile technologies such as phones becoming embedded in people's lives. New innovations such as Googlepay and other payment applications are making mobile phones more important. It is likely that in the future mobile phones will be used for most services. In addition, mobile technology has been linked to the internet of things in which electronic devices are all connected. This means that technology affects everyday life in a way that makes it integral to societal advancement.

Across the debate about the way technology is affecting society has been a common theme around how technology creates entrepreneurial opportunities. As entrepreneurship involves doing something new and changing the status quo it is important to reflect on what this means for society (Ratten, 2014). Entrepreneurship can create wealth but at the same time widen wealth gaps. To add value to society technology needs to be progressive but also cognisant about the need to create a more level playing field amongst citizens. Bruyat and Julien (2000: 173) state that entrepreneurship "is concerned first and foremost with a process of change, emergence and creation: Creation of new value and at the same time change and creation for the individual". This means that technology innovation to lead to entrepreneurship needs to create something different to what has been done in the past. Some experimentation is needed in this process to assess what does and does not work. The creation of new value is at the heart of entrepreneurship and this can be achieved by incorporating feedback and suggestions from consumers. With the rise of mobile communication, real time feedback is becoming more common and can help quicken the entrepreneurship process. This will enable more societal forms of entrepreneurship to develop that stress the need for a more holistic understanding of entrepreneurship.

A range of people and entities is needed for technological progress to lead to entrepreneurial business ventures. Entrepreneurship is carried out by a range of people who all share the common goal of creating new opportunities. Markets can be consumer, business or government orientated so the technological innovation can be applied in the right way. Due to the usefulness of some technology being hard to assess straight away, there can be a degree of uncertainty involved. After the technology has been introduced, modified and accepted in the market then better decisions about its design can be made. This will involve deciding on what kind of resources to use.

Frugal forms of technology innovation require few resources and are developed on an ad-hoc basis. This has been important in enabling poorer consumers access to technology services at cheaper prices. For this reason, frugal innovation has been championed in developing countries as a way to reduce inequality. As there are a large number of people living on subsistence wages it is important that they have access to technology. The concept of frugal innovation in terms of innovating in resource constrained environments has also become popular in developed economies. This has coincided with the maker movement in which more people make their own products. Thus, there is a conundrum in terms of people using high technology devices but at the same time wanting to hand make goods. This is interesting as much of the emphasis on technology innovation has stressed the use of artificial intelligence and less reliance on human interaction. However, at the same time increasingly people are wanting both technology and human involvement in their decisions.

To better understand the role of inequality in society it is important to focus on the context. There are different contexts from geographical to psychological that impact on entrepreneurial behaviours. Whilst context has been taken for granted in entrepreneurship research it is gaining traction as it is an important environmental factor. Context is dynamic as it changes depending on the time period and atmosphere. As Garud, Gehman, and Giuliani (2014: 1177) states "contexts are key moderators of success or failure, dictating the availability or the viability of entrepreneurial innovation". Contexts that are conducive to entrepreneurship have a positive effect on new business formation. This helps build an entrepreneurial ecosystem that is based on technological progression. Contexts that are not good for entrepreneurship tend to value the status quo and not want to change.

As entrepreneurship is a social phenomenon an understanding of contexts is required. The nature and location of individuals and businesses in an area will affect the contextual environment for entrepreneurship. As Wallevik (2016: 12) states there is a "need to analyse entrepreneurship in each specific context to understand: what entrepreneurship is, who the entrepreneur is, where entrepreneurship happens, why entrepreneurship is important, and how one can nurture entrepreneurship". In order to motivate more people to examine inequality, the role of context needs to be emphasised in research. Whilst a consensus about inequality related phenomena remains a distant goal, an emphasis on entrepreneurship and technology innovation will help to fill the research gap on this topic. Current entrepreneurship theories have unquestionably resulted from a focus on understanding the effects of inequality.

## 3 Practical Implications

This book encourages managers to adjust their business strategies to address inequality. Whilst more emphasis on achieving technology breakthroughs is needed, managers need to allocate effort to alleviate the disparity between rich and poor in society. In order to improve society encouraging ways that entrepreneurship can lessen the inequality is needed. The reasons for inequality from technology are complex and varied. Some inequality is created by environmental conditions such as lack of access to transport services. In addition, structural inefficiencies and a reluctance to invest in new business may result in inequality.

Inequality can be lessened when there are spillovers in the form of technology or knowledge, which are important in facilitating the flow of information in the marketplace. Technology spillovers occur when information created by others is obtained without compensation. Some spillovers are embedded in the market as the process takes place from the purchasing or selling of information. In addition, the process of knowledge spillovers involves accessing information that has a potential benefit to the recipient through the exchanging of useful information that can lead to further innovation. Knowledge spillovers are important in markets as they help encourage competitiveness and identifying the magnitude of inequality from technological progress is a major contribution to the policy debate around entrepreneurship.

## 4 Contributions to Theory

The chapters in this book contribute to the literature on technology progress in three main ways. First, an interdisciplinary view on technology innovation is taken that may be relevant for an understanding about the effect of context on entrepreneurship. In some contexts, technology relies on government funding and this may be a crucial factor in ensuring equality. Some countries place a high level of importance on technology as evident in the number of technology companies, students studying science and the resulting entrepreneurial ecosystem. For this reason, theories need to incorporate a contextual element in studies about technological progress. Well known regions for technology innovation such as Silicon Valley have seen a high level of entrepreneurship but mostly related to technology. This has created a gap between those working in the technology sector and those in ancillary services.

Second, the chapters accentuate the fact that there are different ways technology can progress depending on the situation. Some technology at the end of its product lifecycle may be deemed as worthless and undervalued. This can lead to growth in other technology sectors that is more favoured such as in emerging industries. Artificial intelligence and the use of robots in the workplace has been emphasised as a factor leading to inequality in society. This has resulted in a new industrial revolution whereby automation is becoming more evident. At the same time technology that has a social value is more appreciated. This is reflected in the need for more technological services that help older people due to the ageing population in many developed countries. Thus, in emerging or developing countries there is a younger population whilst in developed countries there has been an increase in the number of older people. This can mean some synergies in the use of technology services but at the same time impede progress due to government policy focusing on certain demographic segments.

Third, the chapters synthesize work on technological progress by taking an innovation and entrepreneurship perspective. As the literature on technological progress is still in its early stages, there is some limitations in available research. This means more specific work is required on new technologies that have only just been developed. This will uncover ways that technological progress may be decreasing the inequality in society. It is important to supplement this research with anecdotal evidence about technology practices. Thereby, helping to understand how technology creates inequality.

# 5 Conclusion

With this book, I hope to encourage dialogue from innovation and entrepreneurship scholars about technological progress and inequality. This will shed light on how society is changing and can inform policy. The lack of theory combining technological progress with inequality research means the effect of innovation is often unknown. This can lead to a tendency to overestimate positive or negative effects. This book will serve to highlight areas of potential for future research on inequality. The effect of inequality can only be truly understood by taking a holistic approach to technological innovation. However, there are still gaps in the research about technological progress and inequality that still need to be filled. Examples of questions needing answers regarding inequality and technological innovation include:

- How are different forms of technology affecting inequality in society?
- How do geographic regions and government policy regarding technology affect inequality?
- What are the causes of inequality from technological innovation?
- How does entrepreneurial policy influence technological progress?

A wide range of topics related to inequality are addressed in this book. This book will help practitioners, policy makers and researchers to understand the research on inequality and entrepreneurship. By reading the chapters in this book, there can be new trends identified that pave the way for an alternative way of looking at entrepreneurship to emerge. I advocate in this book more emphasis on inequality in entrepreneurship and technology innovation research. Due to the important social implications of inequality, this book has major implications for entrepreneurship and technological innovation research. I hope this book will stimulate discussion about inequality that will lead to the ongoing advancement of entrepreneurship research.

## References

Bruyat, C., & Julien, P. (2000). Defining the field of research in entrepreneurship. *Journal of Business Venturing, 16*(2), 165–180.

Ferreira, J., Fernandes, C., & Ratten, V. (2015). International entrepreneurship research: Mapping and cognitive structures. *International Journal of Entrepreneurship and Small Business, 30*(4), 545–566.

Ferreira, J. J., & Ratten, V. (2017). Competitiveness of locations: The effects of regional innovation and entrepreneurial practices. *Competitiveness Review, 28*(1), 2–5.

Ferreira, J., Ratten, V., & Dana, L. (2017). Knowledge based spillovers and strategic entrepreneurship. *International Entrepreneurship and Management Journal, 13*(1), 161–167.

Garud, R., Gehman, J., & Giuliani, A. (2014). Contextualising entrepreneurial innovation: A narrative perspective. *Research Policy, 43*, 1177–1188.

Jones, P., Jones, A., Williams-Burnett, N., & Ratten, V. (2017). Let's get physical: Stories of entrepreneurial activity from sports coaches/instructors. *International Journal of Entrepreneurship and Innovation, 18*(4), 219–230.

Parente, R., El Tarabishy, A., Vesci, M., & Botti, A. (2018). The epistemology of humane entrepreneurship: Theory and proposal for future research agenda. *Journal of Small Business Management, 56*(s1), 30–52.

Ratten, V. (2014). Encouraging collaborative entrepreneurship in developing countries: The current challenges and a research agenda. *Journal of Entrepreneurship in Emerging Economics, 6*(3), 298–308.

Ratten, V. (2015). Cloud computing technology innovation advances: A set of research propositions. *International Journal of Cloud Applications and Computing, 5*(1), 71–78.

Ratten, V. (2016). Continuance use intention of cloud computing: Innovativeness and creativity perspectives. *Journal of Business Research, 69*(5), 1737–1740.

Ratten, V., Ferreira, J. J., & Fernandes, C. I. (2017). Innovation management – Current trends and future directions. *International Journal of Innovation and Learning, 22*(2), 135–155.

Ratten, V., & Tajeddini, K. (2017). Women's entrepreneurship and internationalization: Patterns and trends. *International Journal of Sociology and Social Policy, 38*(9/10), 780–793.

Tajeddini, K., Altinay, L., & Ratten, V. (2017). Service innovativeness and the structuring of organizations: The moderating roles of learning orientation and inter-functional coordination. *International Journal of Hospitality Management, 65*, 100–114.

Wallevik, K. (2016). The future of entrepreneurship: Concept and context. In H. Kaufmann (Ed.), *Entrepreneurial challenges in the 21$^{st}$ century* (pp. 12–23). London: Macmillan.

# Transformative Changes and Developments of the Coworking Model: A Narrative Review

**Marko Orel and Ondřej Dvouletý**

**Abstract** Modern times have seen an emergence of new type of office spaces. Coworking spaces are commonly viewed as hybridised workspaces that are not solely perceived as optimal places to work, but as a source of social support for independent professionals and as physical entities that sprung the creation of collaborative communities. These spaces facilitate interactional effects with the use of mediation mechanisms and through serendipitous encounters with individuals from outside of one's own social circle. By co-constructing a sense of community, these environments have reshuffled the flexible work practice and are significantly impacting the lives of flexible workers across the globe. The chapter presents a narrative review of available resources framing historical development of the flexible workspaces and their evolvement into the contemporary coworking environments. The chapter also highlights the role of collaborative workspaces in the modern economy and it proposes challenges for future research.

**Keywords** Coworking · Workspace transformation · Collaborative office · Flexible workspaces · Sustainability · Work individualisation

## 1 Introduction

In the first days of May 2019, CNN published an article describing how WeWork, a multi-billion American company that provides shared workspaces, had morphed into the world's largest physical network of flexible office space users. Due to its fast growth and rapid expansion, the company is not just known for the development of flexible office spaces but also, its leadership in how individuals adapt modern working lifestyles (O'Brien, 2019). Trademarking motivational phrases such as

---

M. Orel (✉) · O. Dvouletý
Department of Entrepreneurship, Faculty of Business Administration, University of Economics, Prague, Czech Republic
e-mail: marko.orel@vse.cz; ondrej.dvoulety@vse.cz

© Springer Nature Switzerland AG 2020
V. Ratten (ed.), *Technological Progress, Inequality and Entrepreneurship*, Studies on Entrepreneurship, Structural Change and Industrial Dynamics,
https://doi.org/10.1007/978-3-030-26245-7_2

*"Thank God it's Monday"* and constructing co-living condos and developing educational facilities, WeWork pivoted from the community-oriented office provider to the global trendsetter of societal changes. It is an indicator of the growing demand for all-inclusive ecosystems that not only affected how people work, but how they live their lives.

Indeed, societal changes and technological advancements now individualise the world of work (McGuigan, 2010; Taylor & Luckman, 2018) and digitalise the modern society (Grantham & Tsekouras, 2004; Valenduc & Vendramin, 2017; van Meel & Vos, 2001). Highly specialised workers tend to be location-independent and work on a flexible basis, frequently changing the location of their work (Baitenizov, Dubina, Campbell, Carayannis, & Azatbek, 2019; Bögenhold & Klinglmair, 2016; Burke, 2015; Kitching & Smallbone, 2012; Spinuzzi, 2012). While flexible work arrangements such as increased feeling of personal control over schedule and work environment are associated with a handful of positive aspects (Kelly & Moen, 2007; Richman, Civian, Shannon, Jeffrey Hill, & Brennan, 2008; Thomas & Ganster, 1995), there are also negative ones that may place significant impact on worker's life. Alienation (Camps & Luna-Arocas, 2009; Sarros, Tanewski, Winter, Santora, & Densten, 2002; Vickers & Parris, 2007), blurring the work-life balance (Desrochers, Hilton, & Larwood, 2005; Fleetwood, 2007; Moen, 2011; Tausig & Fenwick, 2001) and deterioration of social life (Deranty, 2008; Pedersen & Lewis, 2012) are commonly identified as some of the more notable downsides of work individualisation.

With the increase of ranks in the amount of flexible and independent workers, a new type of office spaces started to emerge (Babb, Curtis, & McLeod, 2018). Addressed nowadays as coworking spaces, these modern hybrid workspaces (Marchegiani & Arcese, 2018) are not solely perceived as optimal places to work, but as a source of social support for independent professionals (Gerdenitsch, Scheel, Andorfer, & Korunka, 2016) and as physical entities that sprung the creation of collaborative communities (Rus & Orel, 2015). Coworking spaces facilitate interactional effects (Brown, 2017) through serendipitous encounters with people from outside of one's own organisation, team, and social circle (Spreitzer, Garrett, & Bacevice, 2015). Within these environments, the interaction between groups of individuals is carried out according to predetermined and foreseeable patterns (Orel & Kubátová, 2019). Living spaces within these coworking places promote community processes through loosely structured and predominantly informal interactions (Leclercq-Vandelannoitte & Isaac, 2016). By co-constructing a sense of community at work (Garrett, Spreitzer, & Bacevice, 2017), these environments have reshuffled the flexible work practice (De Peuter, Cohen, & Saraco, 2017) and are significantly impacting the lives of flexible workers across the globe (Bouncken, Laudien, Fredrich, & Görmar, 2018; Butcher, 2018; Kubátová, 2014).

Entis (2019) recently addressed these societal changes and the role of flexible work environments in tackling the collective social void of feeling adrift in which a lack of a sense of community between modern knowledge workers has emerged as *"the big business of loneliness"*. There are more and more flexible workspaces and hybrid ecosystems that are selling human connections and shaping modern workers' lives (Gandini, 2016; Matsushita, 2016). It would be, however, false to conclude that flexible office spaces environments have only recently become the ecosystems that are integrating and interlacing various spheres of an individual's life. Evidently, the evolution of flexible office environments can be earmarked to the nineteenth century due to work automation, but only at the turn of the twentieth century did the working population begin to significantly migrate from industrial environments to the administratively-centred office spaces which in turn affected their social lives (David, 2015; Giuliano, 1982; Manyika et al., 2017). The interpersonal interaction and collaborative involvement in working processes gained significance throughout the last century. A review looking into the transition to an open office environment, and its interaction mechanisms are important to create a better understanding of modern working spaces in the twenty-first century (Klein, DeRouin, & Salas, 2006).

By 2019, an increasing amount of academic research had been conducted on the various aspects of coworking and similar types of flexible office spaces (Bianchi, Casnici, & Squazzoni, 2018; Brown, 2017; De Peuter et al., 2017; Garrett et al., 2017; Gerdenitsch et al., 2016; Han, 2013; Lumley, 2014; Ross & Ressia, 2015; Rus & Orel, 2015; Spinuzzi, 2012; Surman, 2013; Waters-Lynch & Potts, 2017; Winkler, Saltzman, & Yang, 2018). However, by this date, the historical development of coworking model is still unresearched, and has yet to be discussed namely from the perspective of its influence on societal and transformative changes in modern societies.

Therefore, there is a demanding, and critical approach that should be taken toward the creation of a comprehensive overview of the development of coworking spaces. A mere descriptive overview of the development of coworking spaces would be insufficient, as several forms of collaborative workspaces appeared in history—especially towards the end of the twentieth and in the first decade of the twenty-first century—requiring appropriate classification and consequently a distinction with a modern understanding of the model.

This narrative review of the literature analyses the available sources that frame historical development of the flexible workspaces and their evolvement into the contemporary coworking environments. The chapter aims to provide structured overview of the topic for both, research community, stakeholders and professionals interested in coworking, and collaborative workspaces. The chapter also offers several directions for future research.

## 2 Towards Collaborative Use of Workspace

### 2.1 *Human Need for Community*

Formica (2016) argued that communities similar to the coworking spaces of today existed in Renaissance era Florence in the form of early homogenous communities that had specific patterns of work processes and interpersonal relations. There, painters, sculptors, and other artists worked together in transdisciplinary workshops called *Bottegas* (Ceccarelli, 2008). Within these spaces, individuals under the mentorship of older and more experienced artists co-created an organisational culture based on the shared values of cooperation and knowledge exchange. The Systematisation of these exchanges formed the hub of innovations and organisational networks in a real physical environment (Canale, Durante, Paci, & Scarpa, 2018). The key result of the development and operation of these spaces was the design of the Renaissance approach towards understanding and solving the various problems that individuals faced. These environments became a safe place for an elaborated development process for creative communities (Munigala, Oinonen, & Ekman, 2018).

Five centuries later, in the nineteenth century, similar collaborative work environments developed in Paris, France. Within the framework of the *La Ruche* building, French and foreign artists resided in common spaces (Timm-Bottos & Reilly, 2015). At the same time, similar work environments were found in local cafés such as *Le Café de Flore* and *Les Deux Magots* in the Paris Saint-Germain-des-Prés district and the *Cabaret Voltaire Zurich* in Switzerland (Moriset, 2014). The latter primarily functioned as a café or social junction for meetings but also offered a meeting point to writers and other creators. These spaces connected these creatives and helped them to develop new styles and expressions of art. On a related note, *The Writers Room* existing in 1970s New York was a similar environment, which, unlike the aforementioned café-styled environment, explicitly defined as a space intended for writers and their co-operation (Jones, Sundsted, & Bacigalupo, 2009). In the case of these cafés, their primary domain was the articulation of homogeneous communities created within the framework of established organisational cultures based on the principles of cooperation and equality between individuals. While their primary function was to offer physical spaces, a preponderance of evidence pointing toward the existence of mechanisms accelerating the interaction between workspace users was not found. At that point in time, neither the moderated nor spontaneous mechanisms typically used to promote the development of interpersonal relations existed.

Given the advancement of the computer as a working tool and the web as a medium of transmission and direct access to content and information in the last two decades of the twentieth century, individual cafés began to respectively upgrade their infrastructure. In doing so, they became more appealing for individuals who were working off-site and needed a computer with a steady internet connection (Salvador, Sherry, & Urrutia, 2005). To this effect, the Seoul, Korea-based *Electronic Café* which opened in 1988 was the first modern cyber-café fulfilling these requirements. Conversely, its first western counterpart was found in *The SFnet Coffeehouse Network* in San Francisco, California which opened its doors in 1991 (Liff & Lægran, 2003).

These early internet cafés featured stationary computers with access to the world wide web even before the popularisation of portable computers. In the context of descriptive analysis, these places can be understood as temporary working environments with pay-as-you-go access to the computer and the web, and simultaneously also as unconnected junctions of individuals who could work remotely (Broughton, Higgins, Hicks, & Cox, 2010; Salvador et al., 2005). The breakthrough technological advances of the late 1990s and the early twenty-first century that enabled the development of portable computers made internet cafes obsolete (Kellerman, 2009).

Today, internet cafés are still strongly present in less developed countries even though they are almost non-existent in the west (Li, Zhang, Lu, Zhang, & Wang, 2014). Throughout their existence, internet or cyber cafés have been often seen as meeting points for community and neighbourhood (Stewart, 2000), and as social and intellectual spaces (Dewey, 2008).

The portability of electronic devices kickstarted the development of the new office space model. In 1989, the first hot-desk location by the name of *Regus* was established in Belgium and allowed mobile individuals to share work and conference facilities. Soon after, they also provided accommodation capacity which conceptually grouped into their business centres (Virginia & Colin, 2001). The spaces under the *Regus* brand name have focused on servicing individuals by providing them a flexible office space for a limited duration of time without the facilitation of networking possibilities which could be borne of relationships and connections between users. Collaborative actions were limited, but there were no implications that this office model established under *Regus* has interfered with individuals' lives and their well-being. Instead, the establishment of serviced office environments has accelerated the development of office intensification strategies with hot-desking and non-territorial workspace seeing a quick popularization amongst teleworkers (Dent & White, 1998; Lizieri, 2003; Sullivan, 2017).

In parallel with the social movements and relevant technological development, the need for specialised spaces with the established organisational culture arose (Fox, Ulgado, & Rosner, 2015; Smith, Fressoli, Abrol, Arond, & Ely, 2016). Moving into the last part of the twentieth century, an emergence of new collaborative spaces and their consequent geographic concentration primarily led to the development of creative centres as hubs of social innovation (Toivonen, 2016). The first space which could be considered the precursor to the modern coworking space, opened in Berlin, Germany in 1995 as the *C-Base* (Lindtner, Hertz, & Dourish, 2014). Hosting predominantly a homogeneous community of individuals working within the field of digital or analogue technologies, the *C-Base* space—still in operation today—can be classified as a hackerspace. It serves as a model of a space where the community puts the collective achievement of the defined goals which can either be a profitable one, or a non-profitable one, in the foreground (Niaros, Kostakis, & Drechsler, 2017). Even though the *C-Base* appears in the literature as the world's first modern hackerspace, some authors, as its predecessor, mention a smaller community in Michigan, USA which began experimenting with new technologies at the *Grand Valley State University* in 1994 (Dousay, 2017).

However, it appears that hacker spaces are generally orientated towards a niche community that is based on a user-led innovation (Capdevila, 2014) and associated with new technologies (Allen & Potts, 2016). As a supportive environment it could be loosely linked to before mentioned *Bottegas*, but cannot be confused with contemporary workspaces that host heterogeneous group of workers and other individuals. One of the first shared work environments that has been perceived as a focal point model of coordination by individuals with various and diverse backgrounds (Waters-Lynch & Potts, 2017) has been Vienna based *Schraubenfabrik* that opened its doors in 2002 (Brübach-Schlickum, 2016). *Schraubenfabrik* did not self-identify as a collaborative workspace but as a community centre for entrepreneurs or, as the centre for the development of an entrepreneurial community (Hartmann, 2016). It has taken the further development of societal changes to spring the creation and establishment of the first coworking spaces.

Until 2005, collaborative office environments have been commonly linked to on-demand infrastructure that enables office hoteling, a flexible and virtual use of selected workspace (Becker, 1999; Davenport & Pearlson, 1998; Leigh, 1996). Interestingly, even before the period of rapid popularization, these workspaces have been sometimes envisioned as places that are accommodating the new economy (Harrison, 2002). But as several authors pointed out towards hospitality and openness of these spaces, collaborative use has been somewhat pushed aside until the term of "coworking" has been coined. Not only increased demand towards these shared workspaces, but new societal changes have sprung the development of new type of office spaces that have pushed knowledge exchange (Parrino, 2015) and social learning (Bilandzic & Foth, 2013) to the new extent. By co-constructing a sense of community at work (Garrett et al., 2017; Rus & Orel, 2015) and curating the "third place" (Brown, 2017), new workspaces with integrated social spaces have co-created a phenomenon of the sharing economy (Bouncken & Reuschl, 2018).

## 3 The Development of the Coworking Model

### *3.1 From Co-workplace and Co-working to Coworking*

While the phenomenon of coworking is becoming increasingly explored, the terminology around remains largely unexplored. In 1999, the American computer software developer Bernard De Koven first proposed the term "coworking". To this regard, De Koven gave a terminological description as the method of participation by individuals who interact with one another without strictly defined or hierarchically-arranged relationships and on the principles of collaboration (Brown, 2017). As part of his development of computer games and programs in collaboration with other developers who either worked independently or joined the team, De Koven saw the link between face-to-face communication and working with online tools. As the development of deeper mutual relationships is essential, individuals require a real, physical environment and tended to work together as equals (Curaoğlu & Demirbaş, 2017). In the following years, the word "coworking" had been used several times but in different contexts. Until referencing the discussed model directly, the term coworking was used to illustrate the sharing of resources between individuals who are connected into the same organisational network. The usage of a dedicated working environment by individual workers has sometimes been referred as "co-workplace", while the lack of a temporary shared working environment can be termed as "office lessness" (Alizadeh, 2012; Goelman, 2004; Han & Kim, 2014; Johnson, 2003; Sellen & Harper, 2003).

At this point in discussion, the commonly incorrect use of the word "coworking" both in popular texts and in academic debates should be noted. In the initial years of development and elaboration of the coworking model, incorrect terminological use was quite a common occurrence. The word "coworking" had been commonly replaced with the word "co-working" which represents a misconception and a departure from the understanding of the model. Instead, the term "co-working" actually denotes the cooperation between individuals who are interconnected with relations within a given organisation and where the individuals are placed in the role of co-workers. The term "coworking" refers to the cooperation and the sharing of the workspace between individuals working independently given mutual relationships formed on the basis of either spontaneous or moderated processes within a temporary-set or a permanent collaborative workspace. In May 2018, the *Associated Press Stylebook* removed the hyphenated version of the term, clearing the often confusing and excessive use of both academic and industry terminology in this field (Meunier, 2018).

In this regard, the first environment characterised as a modern coworking space and manifesting itself as such was inaugurated in August 2005 by Brad Neuberg in San Francisco taking the geographic name *The Spiral Muse* (Andrade, de Rezende Pinto, de Almeida, & Mesquita, 2017; Cabral & Winden, 2016; Spinuzzi, 2015). In the same year, *The Hub* in London, United Kingdom expanded into the global network of *The Impact Hub*, a franchised group of coworking spaces (Waters-Lynch & Potts, 2017). In some accounts of academic research, some state that the first modern coworking space as *The Hat Factory* which opened its doors in 2006 in San Francisco (Shepard, 2018). While Neuberg was also actively involved in the establishment of the latter, *The Hat Factory* opened as a second coworking space directly replacing *The Spiral Muse* but due to financial difficulties, had closed its doors after one year of operation (Merkel, 2015).

Neuberg was recognized as the first individual to link the word "coworking" with the flexible working space and its collaborative use (Capdevila, 2015; Garrett et al., 2017; Johri & Teo, 2018; Josef & Back, 2018; Rus & Orel, 2015; Spinuzzi, 2012). However, there is an unexplored correlation of the term coined previously by De Koven in 1999 and of the term that Neuberg coined in (2005). Neuberg claims that there was no connection between them and that the term he co-authored independently as the most appropriate word describing the conceptual starting point of *The Spiral Muse*. Furthermore, he adds that De Koven's wording has no connection with the then-emerging trend of opening co-operative spaces, but that it merely describes the method of participation of individuals who interact with one another (Neuberg, 2015).

## 3.2 *The Rise of Temporary Workspace Design*

While the first coworking spaces picked up the pace to reach active momentum and broader recognition, it was the movement of individuals who popularised coworking as a model of flexible workspace use (Putra & Agirachman, 2016). In the beginning of 2006, two self-employed Americans and roommates from New York City organised the first one-off gathering of independent workers and named it as a *Jelly* event. The purpose of *Jelly* was to open the doors of their apartment to both acquaintances and strangers who, due to the independent nature of their work from home, were subject to isolation and alienation. The same year *Solos Working Alone Together (SWAT)* began to organise similar events in Chicago with the aim of connecting individuals once or twice a week in one of the pre-selected cafés (Jones et al., 2009). The attraction of both *SWAT* and *Jelly* events was that they were based on the principle of sharing economies based on the sharing of human and material resources amongst individuals (Cohen & Kietzmann, 2014; John, 2013; Taeihagh, 2017).

Due to the unpretentious organisation and promotion through online tools, these collaborative meet-ups gained access to individual stakeholders, and quickly expanded from the US cities first to Europe and then later to other continents (De Guzman & Tang, 2011). The following waypoints have been recognized as necessary to organize a Jelly-style event and widely adopted amongst individuals or organization who hosted open-office gatherings: (a) free access to the world wide web; (b) a central, easily accessible and free location for the meeting; (c) a space with one or more smaller tables serving as a working area; (d) a sufficient number of electric outlets; (e) access to foods in the form of hot and cold drinks, or the possibility for the users to bring the desired food and drinks with them (Heminsley, 2011). The popularisation of these events can be positively linked with the demand for establishing temporary workspaces and collaborative premises. This can be indicated with the organisation of first *European Jelly Week* in 2011, where 48 hosts throughout 14 European countries opened their physical premises for collaborative use (Roolf, 2011). In 2012, the first *Worldwide Jelly Week* was organised, hosted by 223 hosts in 35 countries around the world (Drew, 2013).

The Jelly-style events can be perceived as an indicator of several societal changes that pointed towards reshaping the knowledge work and the rise of work flexibility. First, the organisation of temporary coworking spaces at various locations and the frequency of attendance and visits showed by independent workers the need to create new permanent premises in different European cities. Second, an interest to empower independently-operating individuals and smaller teams were identified. Last but not least, the developments of a form of digital and creative tourism which would enable independent workers to facilitate the transition (and work) between different existing collaborative spaces were evident (Bouncken, 2018; Jakonen, Kivinen, Salovaara, & Hirkman, 2017; Jones et al., 2009; Orel, 2015; Putra & Agirachman, 2016).

The organisation of either an individual Jelly-style event or that of several interconnected events carried out in series was essential for the further development, and above all, an articulation of the coworking model. These events can be hosted by a person, an existing community or organisation with minimum requirements, making the event feasible and, thanks to its non-profit orientation, easily accessible for a broader range of users. Moreover, the number of visits to the temporarily established collaborative space indicated the need for the establishment of a permanent collaborative workspace (Salovaara, 2015). This represents a predisposition and a starting point for the further development of a shared workspace via a bottom-up approach (Rus & Orel, 2015). Moreover, Jelly-style events represented a real-time promotional platform for individuals or groups, as they could use temporary workspace to establish, and in particular, to strengthen their anticipated relationships with other participants, and incidentally solidifying the level of trust previously already established by digital social networks and similar online tools (Cashman, 2012). Finally, these Jelly-style events were the equivalent of existing peer-to-peer facilities allowing the transfer of knowledge about co-operation as a method of work, which in itself significantly contributed to the spaces' popularization and further development (Heminsley, 2013).

In the first years of its popularisation, Jelly-style events could be understood as a movement toward the creation of heterogeneous communities based on the principles of cooperation and sharing of premises. These collaborative environments were defined as individual accommodation units or dwellings whose tenants can be seen as a smaller community of interconnected individuals which occasionally, and, in exchange for a small fee or some other form of compensation, share the workspace (Putra & Agirachman, 2016; Salovaara, 2015). In the parallel of these events and temporary workspaces, the early coworking model grew primarily based on the common interests of individuals who strove toward the creation of collaboration-based workspaces. The first permanent coworking spaces and their temporary counterparts in the form of *Jelly* events indicated solidarity before the monetisation of related and similar services. In 2008, the US-based workspace *Office Space* established the so-called *Coworking Visa* with its partners to allow the non-payable access of one of the several coworking spaces included in the exchange program. The establishment of this visa helped moderate the process of a user's work flexibility of a particular collaborative space, allowing them to pass between spaces embedded in the program freely and thus interlacing supportive networks (Pohler, 2012; Schuermann, 2014).

## *3.3 Understanding Increased Popularization*

In actuality, the early coworking model was shaped by the communities and by the participation of independently-operating individuals based on the principles of the sharing economy (Hamari, Sjöklint, & Ukkonen, 2016). In particular, the genesis of the collaborative space in this context deviated from other spatially similar ways of organising. Due to its informal and reciprocal organisational culture orientation and the emphasis of cooperation practices similar to those of cooperatives, these spaces are also fundamentally different from (Cabral & Winden, 2016; Iulia Constantinescu & Devisch, 2018). Based on this, we can identify the development of coworking model between 2005 and 2010 as period of genesis for coworking spaces. It was followed by periods of popularisation between 2010 and 2014 and the further hybridisation of the model began in 2014 as an ongoing process.

The first phase of the coworking model development was characterised by a high level of user solidarity from within the co-operative communities, mainly reflected in the mutual assistance and reciprocity demonstrated between users, and the advance (micro) financing of coworking spaces. As noted in the introduction of our discussion, the first collaborative work environments were established in response to the needs of independently working individuals. The solidarity of which was reflected both by providers and users of these places. An example of solidarity is the development of temporary coworking spaces or Jelly-style events, where the organisers of the latter opened the doors of their homes to individuals for one day, thereby blurring the boundary between the work and the home environment. Another well-known example of solidarity is the prepayment of user charges and the creation of space by the method of bootstrapping (*Indy Hall*, Philadelphia) or the accrual of financial support through the leveraging of crowdfunding (*New Work City*, New York).

The leap between the periods of development of the coworking model was marked by two milestones. The first milestone was the reopening of a New York-based coworking space, *New Work City* launched in 2010 with financial resources collected by its users through a crowdfunding campaign. *New Work City* users rebooted a prepayment scheme in the form of a prepaid monthly usage fee and by this they showed their strong identification with space and its agenda (De Guzman & Tang, 2011). The second milestone indicating a leap between two periods and the beginning of the coworking model's broader popularisation was the organisation of the first *Coworking Day* in 2010. This served as the commemoration of the first open modern coworking space *The Spiral Muse*. This *Coworking Day* can be seen as an informally structured international event focused primarily on the promotion of sharing space and the connecting of individuals to the established coworking community within either permanent or temporary coworking spaces globally. Coworking spaces involved in *Coworking day* opened their doors to potential future users as well to the general public for a period of one day each year, and organized events that were in one way or another related to the promotion of sharing (Amador, 2017).

The period of popularisation of the coworking model between 2010 and 2014 was marked by the rapid growth in the number of newly created coworking spaces and the consequent increase in user base. The second half of 2010 brought the estimated number of existing coworking spaces in the world to 600. In 2012, this number grew by 350% to 2072, and then by 215% to 4500 coworking spaces in 2014. By 2015, the number of open coworking spaces was estimated at 7800, which means a further 175% growth (Foertsch, 2016). By the end of 2019, there will presumably be about 21,000 coworking spaces worldwide (Huang, 2019). Given the growth trend and the consideration of other key factors such as (a) fast technological development and the resulting digitization of work; (b) changes in organizations' employment structures; (c) the fluidity of work and the fluctuation of mainly smaller teams; (d) future growth projections of both coworking premises and (e) users are necessary for the needs of further analysis of the model.

The exponential increase in the number of coworking spaces has led to new trends in the model's development. To start, the coworking model became interesting for corporate use (Arora, 2017; Sargent, Cooper, Mellwig, & McDonald, 2018; Spreitzer et al., 2015). This was first indicated by the opening of the *TechHub*, a coworking space opened in 2011 within the *Google Campus* in London, United Kingdom that later branched out to other spaces within five European cities. A similar example can be seen in the already mentioned *WeWork*, the world's fastest growing network of coworking and flexible office spaces with the anticipated growth of opening three to five new locations monthly. The amount of investment capital in this field accelerated and enabled the comprehensive expansion of coworking premises connected into one of the networks. In the case of the *TechHub* franchise, its members can freely move between its franchised spaces. Similarly, *WeWork* persuades members to travel between their coworking spaces (Leclercq-Vandelannoitte & Isaac, 2016). In both cases, the concept of digital tourism is promoted to attract digital nomads or travelling knowledge workers who accelerate the flow of knowledge during their movement between places. The mantra of digital nomadism also encourages individuals to get involved in smaller networks by moving between coworking spaces, thus accelerating the flow of knowledge, increasing the level of mutual participation and affecting faster capital flow (Müller, 2016).

## 3.4 Evolving Trends of the Coworking Model

While fresh capital from investment funds has allowed rapid and exponential growth, and consequently, the acceleration of new coworking spaces being opened, certain positive and negative aspects of swift growth still need to be highlighted. First, the early coworking spaces, both temporary and permanent, were autonomously and commonly bottom-up formed entities, most often co-created and co-financed by their (future) users, resulting in the creation of an organizational culture within a particular space and norms and values mostly based on sharing, co-creation, and collaboration (Spinuzzi, 2015). The pre-financing and integration of potential hegemonic structures instils specific agenda and the particular interests of more substantial stakeholders to directly influence not only the establishment of physical space, thereby circumventing the process of co-creation, but also the establishment of a set of defined acceptance norms (that is, who can use a single space or the preference of the target groups), values (monetization of services before the concept of sharing), and the culture itself.

The briskly growing network of coworking spaces, such as the *WeWork* franchise, can, because of its financial background, open a large number of its branches in a relatively small area or city, and consequently, due to the gap between supply and demand, affect the local coworking space market. The fast growth and concentration of coworking spaces in a particular area and the popularisation of their use indirectly affects the real estate market and socioeconomic changes in that environment while increasing the speed at which gentrification happens (Merkel, 2015). The example of opening new coworking spaces within the *WeWork* franchise in downtrodden and underdeveloped areas of New York suggest a resulting gradual increase in the rental price of both the surrounding business premises and housing units (Babb et al., 2018; Brown, 2017). Consequently, we notice that from 2014 onwards capital investment has increasingly turned to the coworking model as a model for establishing or filling up real-estate capacities (Wright, 2018). From this point of view, in the future, a discussion regarding the influence of coworking environments opened in downtrodden neighbourhoods and its consequent gentrification effect will undoubtedly take place.

The lively popularisation of coworking model in recent years has led away from the heterogeneity of the user community. Consequently, this has resulted in an increasingly dedicated specialisation of premises to address potential customers or users who require a specific and defined working environment (Marchegiani & Arcese, 2018). Nowadays, coworking spaces often strive to optimise the conditions for the formation and the operation of homogeneous coworking communities and adapt to the diversification of the coworking industry. There are specialised coworking spaces for individuals working in the field of culinary arts (Raphael, 2017), for musicians (Di Risio, 2018) and working parents (van Blokland, 2018). Moreover, general coworking spaces are expanding their scope of services in order to increase their competitiveness and positioning on local markets. In addition to office spaces with fixed and flexible work spots, they commonly offer café infrastructure, child care, recreational areas and accommodation units (Halvitigala, Antoniades, & Eves, 2018; Merkel, 2015; Racek, 2015).

This points towards the intensified hybridisation of the model as coworking spaces strive toward recreating habitat that can be referred to as a fourth living place in addition to being a collaborative workspace (Morisson, 2018). We may assume that hybridised coworking spaces will increasingly focus on the localisation of all desired and operational services in one place in order to cover the living, working and social segments of the individual in a comprehensive manner.

## 4 Concluding Remarks

This chapter has comprehensively analysed existing literature and showed that flexible office spaces are rapidly developing and hybridising. Fast growth and development of these places have been commonly connected with socioeconomic changes of the particular period. With the twenty-first century economy being increasingly knowledge and innovation based, and increasingly thriving in dense urban centres the flexible workplaces are seeing past paced transformative changes. From early *Bottegas*, flexible workplaces have morphed first into niche community centres and later on evolved into coworking spaces that are keen to become a part of collaborative work culture.

It appears that there have been significant changes in how knowledge workers interact and collaborate. As explored throughout the chapter, coworking spaces promote more significant innovation and efficiency, allowing the best people for a particular project to come together quickly and affordably with lowering the number of obstructions that would limit the diversity of perspectives and backgrounds of a collaborative community. Shift towards collaborative action orientated workspaces can thus be seen as places that are collectively tackling social void brought upon by new technologies and societal changes. Promoting collective processes through loosely structured and predominantly informal interactions leads towards the co-construction community of work that collectively tackled the challenges and pitfalls of flexible work practice. Moreover, collaborative communities are significantly impacting the lives of flexible workers and enabling them to progress not only with their careers but also raise the quality of their lives.

As coworking spaces are shared by individuals who generally do not work for the same organisation, they tend to break social barriers and interlace individuals in supportive networks. This does not results solely in increased innovation, work efficiency and collaboration, but also causes that involved individuals benefit from received emotional support (Gerdenitsch et al., 2016), reduced alienation and isolation (De Peuter et al., 2017), improved work-life balance (Gandini, 2016), and increased productivity leading to new product and project opportunities (Cabral & Winden, 2016). The vast arrange of positive benefits seem to affect the growing number of coworking spaces around the world, and it does not appear that this trend will slow down within the next couple of years.

Although the phenomenon of the coworking model is receiving increased attention both within the workspace industry, academia and the general public, there are still many fields that will require more attention. The revision of available resources showed that the coworking model is continuing its hybridisation with new types of both independent and franchise spaces emerging and opening their doors. Authors thus propose more focused studies on community development trends within these workplaces and their role in the modern economies.

**Acknowledgement** This work was supported by the Internal Grant Agency of the Faculty of Business Administration, University of Economics in Prague under no. IP300040.

# References

Alizadeh, T. (2012). Teleworkers' characteristics in live/work communities: Lessons from the United States and Australia. *Journal of Urban Technology, 19*(3), 63–84.

Allen, D. W., & Potts, J. (2016). How innovation commons contribute to discovering and developing new technologies. *International Journal of the Commons, 10*(2), 1035–1054.

Amador, C. (2017). *International Coworking Day: The perfect day to set a new world record.* Available at: https://allwork.space/2017/08/international-coworking-day-the-perfect-day-to-set-a-new-world-record/

Andrade, H. D. G. C., de Rezende Pinto, M., de Almeida, G. T., & Mesquita, M. C. (2017). I share, therefore I am? The (re) construction of consumer identity by collaborative con-sumption. *REBRAE, 10*(1), 167–182.

Arora, S. (2017). Changing dynamics of corporate real estate: The rise of coworking spaces. *Corporate Real Estate Journal, 7*(2), 127–136.
Babb, C., Curtis, C., & McLeod, S. (2018). The rise of shared work spaces: A disruption to urban planning policy? *Urban Policy and Research, 36*(4), 496–512.
Baitenizov, D. T., Dubina, I. N., Campbell, D. F., Carayannis, E. G., & Azatbek, T. A. (2019). Freelance as a creative mode of self-employment in a new economy (a literature review). *Journal of the Knowledge Economy, 10*(1), 1–17.
Becker, F. (1999). Beyond alternative officing: Infrastructure on-demand. *Journal of Corporate Real Estate, 1*(2), 154–168.
Bianchi, F., Casnici, N., & Squazzoni, F. (2018). Solidarity as a byproduct of professional collaboration: Social support and trust in a coworking space. *Social Networks, 54*, 61–72.
Bilandzic, M., & Foth, M. (2013). Libraries as coworking spaces: Understanding user motivations and perceived barriers to social learning. *Library Hi Tech, 31*(2), 254–273.
Bögenhold, D., & Klinglmair, A. (2016). Independent work, modern organizations and entrepreneurial labor: Diversity and hybridity of freelancers and self-employment. *Journal of Management & Organization, 22*(6), 843–858.
Bouncken, R. B. (2018). University coworking-spaces: Mechanisms, examples, and suggestions for entrepreneurial universities. *International Journal of Technology Management, 77*(1-3), 38–56.
Bouncken, R. B., Laudien, S. M., Fredrich, V., & Görmar, L. (2018). Coopetition in coworking-spaces: Value creation and appropriation tensions in an entrepreneurial space. *Review of Managerial Science, 12*(2), 385–410.
Bouncken, R. B., & Reuschl, A. J. (2018). Coworking-spaces: How a phenomenon of the sharing economy builds a novel trend for the workplace and for entrepreneurship. *Review of Managerial Science, 12*(1), 317–334.
Broughton, A., Higgins, T., Hicks, B., & Cox, A. (2010). *Workplaces and social networking. The implications for employment relations*. Brighton: Institute for Employment Studies.
Brown, J. (2017). Curating the "third place"? Coworking and the mediation of creativity. *Geoforum, 82*, 112–126.
Brübach-Schlickum, S. (2016). Coworking als alternatives Arbeitsplatzkonzept–Fallstudie Combinat 56. In *Arbeitsplatz der Zukunft* (pp. 273–290). Wiesbaden: Springer Gabler.
Burke, A. (Ed.). (2015). *The handbook of research on freelancing and self-employment*. Dublin: Senate Hall Academic Publishing.
Butcher, T. (2018). Learning everyday entrepreneurial practices through coworking. *Management Learning, 49*(3), 327–345.
Cabral, V., & Winden, W. V. (2016). Coworking: An analysis of coworking strategies for interaction and innovation. *International Journal of Knowledge-Based Development, 7*(4), 357–377.
Camps, J., & Luna-Arocas, R. (2009). High involvement work practices and firm performance. *The International Journal of Human Resource Management, 20*(5), 1056–1077.
Canale, A., Durante, D., Paci, L., & Scarpa, B. (2018). Connecting statistical brains. *Significance, 15*(1), 38–40.
Capdevila, I. (2014, November). How can City labs enhance the citizens' motivation in different types of innovation activities? In *International conference on social informatics* (pp. 64–71). Cham: Springer.
Capdevila, I. (2015). Co-working spaces and the localised dynamics of innovation in Barcelona. *International Journal of Innovation Management, 19*(03), 1–28.
Cashman, A. (2012). *Coworking...served hot: Pop-up coworking spaces*. Available at: http://www.deskmag.com/en/coworking-served-hot-pop-up-coworking-spaces-653
Ceccarelli, M. (2008). Renaissance of machines in Italy: From Brunelleschi to Galilei through Francesco di Giorgio and Leonardo. *Mechanism and Machine Theory, 43*(12), 1530–1542.
Cohen, B., & Kietzmann, J. (2014). Ride on! Mobility business models for the sharing economy. *Organization & Environment, 27*(3), 279–296.

Curaoğlu, F., & Demirbaş, D. (2017). From co-working places to new education places. *The Design Journal, 20*(1), 4765–4767.

Davenport, T. H., & Pearlson, K. (1998). Two cheers for the virtual office. *MIT Sloan Management Review, 39*(4), 51.

David, H. (2015). Why are there still so many jobs? The history and future of workplace automation. *Journal of Economic Perspectives, 29*(3), 3–30.

De Guzman, G. V., & Tang, A. I. (2011). *Working in the unoffice: A guide to coworking for indie workers, small businesses, and nonprofits*. San Francisco, CA: Night Owls Press LLC.

De Peuter, G., Cohen, N. S., & Saraco, F. (2017). The ambivalence of coworking: On the politics of an emerging work practice. *European Journal of Cultural Studies, 20*(6), 687–706.

Dent, P., & White, A. (1998). Corporate real estate: Changing office occupier needs-a case study. *Facilities, 16*(9/10), 262–270.

Deranty, J. P. (2008). Work and the precarisation of existence. *European Journal of Social Theory, 11*(4), 443–463.

Desrochers, S., Hilton, J. M., & Larwood, L. (2005). Preliminary validation of the work-family integration-blurring scale. *Journal of Family Issues, 26*(4), 442–466.

Dewey, B. I. (2008). Social, intellectual, and cultural spaces: Creating compelling library environments for the digital age. *Journal of Library Administration, 48*(1), 85–94.

Di Risio, A. (2018). *Coworking spaces for artists and creatives*. Available at: https://www.coworkingresources.org/blog/coworking-spaces-for-artists-and-creatives

Dousay, T. A. (2017). Defining and differentiating the makerspace (pp. 69-74). Englewood Cliffs, NJ: Educational Technology.

Drew, J. (2013), World Jelly week. *UK Jelly*. Available at: https://www.uk-jelly.org.uk/worldwide-jelly-week/

Entis, L. (2019). The big business of loneliness. *Vox*. Available at: https://www.vox.com/the-highlight/2019/4/29/18511580/loneliness-co-living-coworking-friend-app-tribe-wework

Fleetwood, S. (2007). Why work–life balance now? *The International Journal of Human Resource Management, 18*(3), 387–400.

Foertsch, C. (2016). *2016 Coworking forecast*. Available at: http://www.deskmag.com/en/2016-forecast-global-coworking-survey-results

Formica, P. (2016). *The innovative coworking spaces of 15th-century Italy*. Harvard Business Review Digital Article.

Fox, S., Ulgado, R. R., & Rosner, D. (2015, February). Hacking culture, not devices: Access and recognition in feminist hackerspaces. In *Proceedings of the 18th ACM conference on computer supported cooperative work & social computing* (pp. 56–68). New York, NY: ACM.

Gandini, A. (2016). Coworking: The freelance mode of organisation? In *The reputation economy* (pp. 97–105). London: Palgrave Macmillan.

Garrett, L. E., Spreitzer, G. M., & Bacevice, P. A. (2017). Co-constructing a sense of community at work: The emergence of community in coworking spaces. *Organization Studies, 38*(6), 821–842.

Gerdenitsch, C., Scheel, T. E., Andorfer, J., & Korunka, C. (2016). Coworking spaces: A source of social support for independent professionals. *Frontiers in Psychology, 7*, 581.

Giuliano, V. E. (1982). The mechanization of office work. *Scientific American, 247*(3), 148–165.

Goelman, A. (2004). The co-workplace: Teleworking in the neighborhood/wired to the world, chained to the home: Telework in daily life. *American Planning Association. Journal of the American Planning Association, 70*(1), 108.

Grantham, A., & Tsekouras, G. (2004). Information society: Wireless ICTs' transformative potential. *Futures, 36*(3), 359–377.

Halvitigala, D., Antoniades, H., & Eves, C. (2018, July). *CoWorking culture–challenges and opportunities for office landlords*. In Pacific Rim Real Estate Society Conference. Auckland: PRRES Inc.

Hamari, J., Sjöklint, M., & Ukkonen, A. (2016). The sharing economy: Why people participate in collaborative consumption. *Journal of the Association for Information Science and Technology, 67*(9), 2047–2059.

Han, H. S. (2013). A study on the composition and characteristic of coworking space. *Korean Institute of Interior Design Journal, 22*(5), 276–283.

Han, S., & Kim, M. J. (2014). Discourse analysis on ICT and home-from electronic cottage to sharable home. *Journal of the Korean Housing Association, 25*(3), 115–121.

Harrison, A. (2002). Accommodating the new economy: The SANE space environment model. *Journal of Corporate Real Estate, 4*(3), 248–265.

Hartmann, M. (2016). Coworking oder auch die (De-) Mediatisierung von Arbei. In *Medien-Arbeit im Wandel* (pp. 177–204). Wiesbaden: Springer VS.

Heminsley, J. (2011). *How to Jelly: A guide to casual coworking*. Available at: https://www.shareable.net/blog/how-to-jelly-a-guide-to-casual-coworking

Heminsley, J. (2013). *Why is Jelly good for small business*. Available at: https://www.theguardian.com/small-business-network/2013/may/25/jelly-working-home-meetup-group

Huang, Y. (2019). *Coworking key figures: Data and estimations for 2019*. Available at: https://www.coworkingresources.org/blog/key-figures-coworking-growth

Iulia Constantinescu, T., & Devisch, O. (2018). Portraits of work: Mapping emerging coworking dynamics. *Information, Communication & Society, 21*(9), 1263–1278.

Jakonen, M., Kivinen, N., Salovaara, P., & Hirkman, P. (2017). Towards an economy of encounters? A critical study of affectual assemblages in coworking. *Scandinavian Journal of Management, 33*(4), 235–242.

John, N. A. (2013). Sharing and web 2.0: The emergence of a keyword. *New Media & Society, 15*(2), 167–182.

Johnson, L. C. (2003). *The co-workplace: Teleworking in the neighbourhood*. Vancouver, BC: UBC Press.

Johri, A., & Teo, H. J. (2018, August). Achieving equilibrium through coworking: Work-life balance in FLOSS through multiple spaces and media use. In *Proceedings of the 14th international symposium on open collaboration* (p. 7). New York, NY: ACM.

Jones, D., Sundsted, T., & Bacigalupo, T. (2009). *I'm outta here! How coworking is making the office obsolete*.

Josef, B., & Back, A. (2018, April). Coworking as a new innovation scenario from the perspective of mature organisations. In *International OFEL conference on governance, management and entrepreneurship* (pp. 491–507). Zagreb: Centar za istrazivanje i razvoj upravljanja doo.

Kellerman, A. (2009). The end of spatial reorganization? Urban landscapes of personal mobilities in the information age. *Journal of Urban Technology, 16*(1), 47–61.

Kelly, E. L., & Moen, P. (2007). Rethinking the clockwork of work: Why schedule control may pay off at work and at home. *Advances in Developing Human Resources, 9*(4), 487–506.

Kitching, J., & Smallbone, D. (2012). Are freelancers a neglected form of small business? *Journal of Small Business and Enterprise Development, 19*(1), 74–91.

Klein, C., DeRouin, R. E., & Salas, E. (2006). Uncovering workplace interpersonal skills: A review, framework, and research agenda. *International Review of Industrial and Organizational Psychology, 21*, 79–127.

Kubátová, J. (2014, September). The cause and impact of the development of coworking in the current knowledge economy. In *European conference on knowledge management ECKM* (Vol. 15, pp. 571–577).

Leclercq-Vandelannoitte, A., & Isaac, H. (2016). The new office: How coworking changes the work concept. *Journal of Business Strategy, 37*(6), 3–9.

Leigh, N. G. (1996). Fixed structures in transition: The changing demand for office and industrial infrastructure. In *The transition to flexibility* (pp. 137–153). Boston, MA: Springer.

Li, Y., Zhang, X., Lu, F., Zhang, Q., & Wang, Y. (2014). Internet addiction among elementary and middle school students in China: A nationally representative sample study. *Cyberpsychology, Behavior and Social Networking, 17*(2), 111–116.

Liff, S., & Lægran, A. S. (2003). Cybercafés: Debating the meaning and significance of Internet access in a café environment. *New Media & Society, 5*(3), 307–312.

Lindtner, S., Hertz, G. D., & Dourish, P. (2014, April). Emerging sites of HCI innovation: Hackerspaces, hardware startups & incubators. In *Proceedings of the SIGCHI conference on human factors in computing systems* (pp. 439–448). New York, NY: ACM.

Lizieri, C. M. (2003). Occupier requirements in commercial real estate markets. *Urban Studies, 40*(5–6), 1151–1169.

Lumley, R. M. (2014). A coworking project in the campus library: Supporting and modeling entrepreneurial activity in the academic library. *New Review of Academic Librarianship, 20*(1), 49–65.

Manyika, J., Lund, S., Chui, M., Bughin, J., Woetzel, J., Batra, P., et al. (2017). *Jobs lost, jobs gained: Workforce transitions in a time of automation.* New York, NY: McKinsey Global Institute.

Marchegiani, L., & Arcese, G. (2018). Collaborative spaces and coworking as hybrid workspaces: Friends or foes of learning and innovation? In *Learning and innovation in hybrid organizations* (pp. 51–71). Cham: Palgrave Macmillan.

Matsushita, K. (2016). Mediated workplaces and work styles as second offline. In *The post-mobile society* (pp. 53–62). New York: Routledge.

McGuigan, J. (2010). Creative labour, cultural work and individualisation. *International Journal of Cultural Policy, 16*(3), 323–335.

Merkel, J. (2015). Coworking in the city. *ephemera, 15*(2), 121–139.

Meunier, J. (2018). *After more than a decade, 'co-working' is now officially 'coworking'*. Available at: https://allwork.space/2018/10/after-more-than-a-decade-co-working-is-now-officially-coworking/

Moen, P. (2011). From 'work–family' to the 'gendered life course' and 'fit': Five challenges to the field. *Community, Work & Family, 14*(1), 81–96.

Moriset, B. (2014, January 23–25). *Building new places of the creative economy. The rise of co-working spaces.* Paper presented at the 2nd Geography of Innovation International Conference 2014, Utrecht.

Morisson, A. (2018, May). A typology of places in the knowledge economy: Towards the fourth place. In *International symposium on new metropolitan perspectives* (pp. 444–451). Cham: Springer.

Müller, A. (2016). The digital nomad: Buzzword or research category? *Transnational Social Review, 6*(3), 344–348.

Munigala, V., Oinonen, P., & Ekman, K. (2018). Envisioning future innovative experimental ecosystems through the foresight approach. Case: Design factory. *European Journal of Futures Research, 6*(1), 1.

Neuberg, B. (2005). *Coworking – Community for developers who work from home.* Available at: http://codinginparadise.org/weblog/2005/08/coworking-community-for-developers-who.html

Neuberg, B. (2015). *The start of coworking (from the guy that started it).* Available at: http://codinginparadise.org/ebooks/html/blog/start_of_coworking.html

Niaros, V., Kostakis, V., & Drechsler, W. (2017). Making (in) the smart city: The emergence of makerspaces. *Telematics and Informatics, 34*(7), 1143–1152.

O'Brien, S.A. (2019). WeWork isn't just selling desk space. It's selling a new way of life. *CNN Business.* Available at: https://edition.cnn.com/2019/05/03/tech/wework-culture/index.html

Orel, M. (2015). Working in co working spaces: The social and economic engagement of European youth. *Perspectives on youth, 2,* 133–139.

Orel, M., & Kubátová, J. (2019). Coworking as a model for conscious business. *Journal of Global Responsibility.*

Parrino, L. (2015). Coworking: Assessing the role of proximity in knowledge exchange. *Knowledge Management Research & Practice, 13*(3), 261–271.

Pedersen, V. B., & Lewis, S. (2012). Flexible friends? Flexible working time arrangements, blurred work-life boundaries and friendship. *Work, Employment and Society, 26*(3), 464–480.

Pohler, N. (2012). Neue Arbeitsräume für neue Arbeitsformen: Coworking spaces. *Österreichische Zeitschrift für Soziologie, 37*(1), 65–78.
Putra, G. B., & Agirachman, F. A. (2016). Urban coworking space: Creative tourism in digital nomads perspective. In *Proceedings of Arte-Polis 6 international conference* (pp. 169–178).
Racek, M. H. F. (2015). Coworking spaces in Slovakia. *Management Review, 9*(2), 29–43.
Raphael, R. (2017). *WeWork for chefs: How one coworking incubator fuels food innovation.* Available at: https://www.fastcompany.com/40457426/wework-for-chefs-how-one-co-working-incubator-fuels-food-innovation
Richman, A. L., Civian, J. T., Shannon, L. L., Jeffrey Hill, E., & Brennan, R. T. (2008). The relationship of perceived flexibility, supportive work–life policies, and use of formal flexible arrangements and occasional flexibility to employee engagement and expected retention. *Community, work and family, 11*(2), 183–197.
Roolf, A. (2011). Results of Europe's first Jelly week. *Deskmag.* Available at: http://www.deskmag.com/en/results-of-europes-first-jelly-week-coworking-172
Ross, P., & Ressia, S. (2015). Neither office nor home: Coworking as an emerging workplace choice. *Employment Relations Record, 15*(1), 42.
Rus, A., & Orel, M. (2015). Coworking: A community of work. *Teorija in Praksa, 52*(6), 1017–1038.
Salovaara, P. (2015). What can the coworking movement tell us about the future of workplaces. In *Leadership in spaces and places* (pp. 27–48). Northampton, MA: Edward Elgar.
Salvador, T., Sherry, J. W., & Urrutia, A. E. (2005). Less cyber, more café: Enhancing existing small businesses across the digital divide with ICTs. *Information Technology for Development, 11*(1), 77–95.
Sargent, K., Cooper, J., Mellwig, B., & McDonald, M. (2018). Coworking and the disruption of the current corporate real estate model. *Corporate Real Estate Journal, 7*(3), 267–276.
Sarros, J. C., Tanewski, G. A., Winter, R. P., Santora, J. C., & Densten, I. L. (2002). Work alienation and organizational leadership. *British Journal of Management, 13*(4), 285–304.
Schuermann, M. (2014). *Coworking space: A potent business model for plug 'n play and indie workers.* Epublication.
Sellen, A. J., & Harper, R. H. (2003). *The myth of the paperless office.* Cambridge, MA: MIT.
Shepard, J. M. (2018). Understanding co-working with the growth and development of freelancers. *Management and Organizational Studies, 5*(2), 1.
Smith, A., Fressoli, M., Abrol, D., Arond, E., & Ely, A. (2016). *Grassroots innovation movements.* New York, NY: Routledge.
Spinuzzi, C. (2012). Working alone together: Coworking as emergent collaborative activity. *Journal of Business and Technical Communication, 26*(4), 399–441.
Spinuzzi, C. (2015). *All edge: Inside the new workplace networks.* Chicago: University of Chicago Press.
Spreitzer, G., Garrett, L., & Bacevice, P. (2015). Should your company embrace coworking? *MIT Sloan Management Review, 57*(1), 27.
Stewart, J. (2000). Cafematics: The cybercafe and the community. In *Community informatics: Enabling communities with information and communications technologies* (pp. 320–338). Hershey, PA: IGI Global.
Sullivan, J. (2017). Considering employee needs during a catastrophe requires innovative recovery plans: Why traditional workplace recovery solutions are outdated. *Journal of Business Continuity & Emergency Planning, 10*(3), 259–267.
Surman, T. (2013). Building social entrepreneurship through the power of coworking. *Innovations: Technology, Governance, Globalization, 8*(3-4), 189–195.
Taeihagh, A. (2017). Crowdsourcing, sharing economies and development. *Journal of Developing Societies, 33*(2), 191–222.
Tausig, M., & Fenwick, R. (2001). Unbinding time: Alternate work schedules and work-life balance. *Journal of Family and Economic Issues, 22*(2), 101–119.

Taylor, S., & Luckman, S. (2018). Collection introduction: The 'new normal' of working lives. In *The new normal of working lives* (pp. 1–15). Cham: Palgrave Macmillan.

Thomas, L. T., & Ganster, D. C. (1995). Impact of family-supportive work variables on work-family conflict and strain: A control perspective. *Journal of Applied Psychology, 80*(1), 6.

Timm-Bottos, J., & Reilly, R. C. (2015). Learning in third spaces: Community art studio as storefront university classroom. *American Journal of Community Psychology, 55*(1-2), 102–114.

Toivonen, T. (2016). What is the social innovation community? Conceptualizing an emergent collaborative organization. *Journal of Social Entrepreneurship, 7*(1), 49–73.

Valenduc, G., & Vendramin, P. (2017). Digitalisation, between disruption and evolution. *Transfer: European Review of Labour and Research, 23*(2), 121–134.

van Blokland, A. B. (2018). *London's hottest coworking spaces have childcare for your kids*. Available at: https://www.forbes.com/sites/anettebvanblokland/2018/07/17/londons-hottest-coworking-spaces-have-childcare-for-your-kids/#3e9c04bd7631

van Meel, J., & Vos, P. (2001). Funky offices: Reflections on office design in the 'new economy'. *Journal of Corporate Real Estate, 3*(4), 322–334.

Vickers, M. H., & Parris, M. A. (2007). "Your job no longer exists!": From experiences of alienation to expectations of resilience—A phenomenological study. *Employee Responsibilities and Rights Journal, 19*(2), 113–125.

Virginia, G., & Colin, L. (2001). Friction and inertia: Business change, corporate real estate portfolios and the UK office market. *Journal of Real Estate Research, 22*(1-2), 59–80.

Waters-Lynch, J., & Potts, J. (2017). The social economy of coworking spaces: A focal point model of coordination. *Review of Social Economy, 75*(4), 417–433.

Winkler, C., Saltzman, E., & Yang, S. (2018). Improvement of practice in entrepreneurship education through action research: The case of coworking at a nonresidential college. *Entrepreneurship Education and Pedagogy, 1*(2), 139–165.

Wright, D. (2018). Match made in heaven: Investment benefits of coworking spaces in historic sacred places. *Cornell Real Estate Review, 16*(1), 50–61.

# The Role of ICT in Involving the Tourist and in Sustainability of Tourism Destinations

Célia M. Q. Ramos, Georgette Andraz, and Irene Cardoso

**Abstract** A tourist destination, in addition, to attracting tourists, both national and international, must take care of the interests of the local community in order to obtain economic development, improve the quality of life of the resident and meet the satisfaction of visitors. The quality of experiences perceived by tourists, about a tourist destination, contributes to their satisfaction and to the creation of richer memories. In this context, the role of Information and Communication Technologies (ICTs) can be the way to improve and add value to the experience, through the involvement of tourists and residents, taking into account the search made by tourists about their tourist destination before and during travel, through the dissemination of its authenticity, values and heritage of the destination by other tourists, residents and by official destination management organizations. The present research intends to analyse the role played by ICT to improve the competitiveness of the destination, in order to meet the needs of tourists, taking in consideration the quality of life of its residents. The methodology used considers descriptive statistical analysis and non-parametric tests applied to research questions. The research concluded that tourists use ICT at any time during their travel, both in planning and in the consumption phase, and that they use the technology in order to find information on the destination, make reservations and share their experiences on the social networks.

**Keywords** Consumer behaviour · Sustainability · Tourism destination management · Tourism experience · Social media marketing · Information and communication technologies (ICT)

---

C. M. Q. Ramos (✉)
ESGHT, CIEO & CEFAGE, Universidade do Algarve, Faro, Portugal
e-mail: cmramos@ualg.pt

G. Andraz
ESGHT & CEFAGE, Universidade do Algarve, Faro, Portugal
e-mail: gandraz@ualg.pt

I. Cardoso
ISEG, Lisbon, Portugal
e-mail: irene.cardoso@iseg.ulisboa.pt

## 1 Introduction

Tourism is currently one of the largest economic activities with the highest growth rate worldwide (Tahayori & Moharrer, 2006). In a global world, where travel is increasingly easy and accessible, tourist destinations are increasingly competitive to attract tourists, businesses and investments. However, the management of tourism destination should consider several functions that contribute to the success and attract tourist to visit their space (Bornhorst, Ritchie, & Sheehan, 2010).

As tourism is an information-intensive industry (Benckendorff, Xiang, & Sheldon, 2019), the widespread use of information and communication technologies (ICT) has played a relevant role in both the supply and demand side (Oliveira & Panyik, 2015). In the search perspective, ICT, particularly social networks, allows immediate access to relevant information about destinations, sharing experiences after and during consumption of the tourist product, photos, among others (Xiang & Gretzel, 2010). There is evidence that almost all tourist uses ICT to obtain information about the tourism destination.

Tourism destinations consist of a set of interrelated and interdependent products and services that are part of the tourism system which is difficult to manage (Fyall, 2011). The variety, complementarity, interconnection and interdependence of products and services, which characterize tourism activity in a tourist destination, cause fragmentations that make it difficult to manage the destination (Boes, Buhalis, & Inversini, 2015).

The challenges posed to the organizations that manage the destinations go through the management and control of critical resources known as the six A's (attractions, accessibility, amenities, available packages, activities, ancillary services) while simultaneously increasing the profit and benefits for the destination (Boes et al., 2015; Murphy, Pritchard, & Smith, 2000), as well as to guarantee the quality and maintenance of the different values and cultures that coexist in the population, in order to reduce impacts among all actors. For this system to function successfully, it must satisfy the potential customer who is the tourist, who only has access to information of different formats (text, photographs, and videos) to choose and acquire a tourist product associated with a tourist destination.

Managing the system and managing the associated information in order to engage the tourist is only possible with innovative technologies, where information from local and global agents, from public and private companies, coexists with a view to increasing the tourist satisfaction when finally consuming the product tourism. All this in order to transform the tourist destinations as a "places utilizing the available technological tools and techniques to enable demand and supply to co-create value, pleasure, and experiences for the tourist and wealth, profit, and benefits for the organizations and the destination" (Boes et al., 2015: 394), where concerns about competitiveness, sustainability, and inclusiveness on the concept of providing holistic Smart Tourism Destinations are present (Buhalis & Amaranggana, 2015; Gössling & Michael Hall, 2019).

The present research intends to analyse the relevance of ICTs to improve the competitiveness of the tourism destination, in order to meet the needs of tourists by one side, and guarantee the sustainability, taking in consideration concerns about the life quality of their residents.

Following the introduction, the chapter is subdivided into three sections: the first presents the concepts and challenges associated to the management of tourism destination conjugated with information and communication technologies, considering the role, influence and potentialities to add value to the touristic experience of the visitors. The second section presents the methodology used in the study. The third section gives the results of the study taking into consideration descriptive statistical analysis and non-parametric tests applied to research questions. Finally, some conclusions, limitations and future research paths are drawn about the investigation presented in this chapter.

## 2 Management of Tourism Destination and ICT

A tourism destination should acquire centrality, in a way to achieve interest as a territory that travellers want to visit, should meet customer satisfaction through a structured offer of services, availability and sharing of resources and attractions, so that the visitor can experience the visit and make combinations according to their preferences (Bornhorst et al., 2010; Giménez, 2006). At the same time, must have a brand that attractively translates the offer, facilitates its identification and gives rise to an idea of the interaction of affections and feelings.

It must adopt a form of joint marketing, with vertical marketing cooperation for the whole space that defines the tourism destination (Damayanti, Scott, & Ruhanen, 2017), which interlinks the stakeholders and should integrate the sustainability concerns to achieve a better and more sustainable future for all, in accordance with the objectives of the United Nations (2019).

A tourist destination includes urban, social and cultural structures, among others, aiming at achieving the best quality of residents and attracting tourists, with the objective of achieving economic development superior to what it would achieve by means of other factors of production (Giménez, 2006), while define and apply rules to achieve the sustainability concerns (Ritchie & Crouch, 2003), as presented in the Fig. 1.

According to Fig. 1, in the management of tourist destinations, five functions should be considered in order to achieve a holistic or integrated management: international competitiveness, economic development, quality of life, satisfaction and sustainability concerns.

International competitiveness is one of the most important function in the integrated management of tourist destinations (Boes et al., 2015), it aims at attracting foreign capital to the region, exporting the tourism product, developing strategies to attract attention and attracting tourists at an international level.

Economic development results from the influx of tourists attracted to visit the tourist destination, which consequently contributes to: (i) the development of businesses located at the destination, both private and public, with a view to increasing their economic profitability; (ii) the development of adequate infrastructure, increased employment, which will improve the social profitability of residents;

(iii) the conditioning the more marked maintenance needs associated with the territory and the heritage, thus increasing its value and authenticity, which will lead to an environmental profitability (Chen, 2015).

Quality of life is related to how space is used by residents and tourists to live, to develop relationships, to produce new products complementary to tourism, to create and develop cultural and identity values, to create entertainment activities, among other aspects related to the people who enjoy the space (Uysal, Sirgy, Woo, & Kim, 2016).

Satisfaction links the three functions mentioned above with a view to developing experiences that contribute to the satisfaction of all stakeholders in the tourism system: tourists, residents, businesses and other stakeholders.

However, today, sustainability concerns must be considered as a fifth functions to be considered in the management of destinations, since they condition the four previous axes. The challenges related to poverty, inequality, climate, environmental degradation, prosperity and peace and justice are interlinked (United Nations, 2019), related to all actors, from the tourist to the resident, through all the players in the tourist distribution chain.

Taking into account the five functions presented in Fig. 1, the success of the management of a tourist destination will depend on all the actors in each function and the relationship between the processes associated with each one, since an inefficient cooperation can put in question the attractiveness of the destination, diminishing its potential to attract visitors, which will jeopardize its competitiveness. However, the success of the development and management of a tourist destination also depends on the use of ICT (Giménez, 2006), which can contribute not only to support the decision-making of the tourist, but also to the control and management of tourism resources and also to influence the value of tourism experiences.

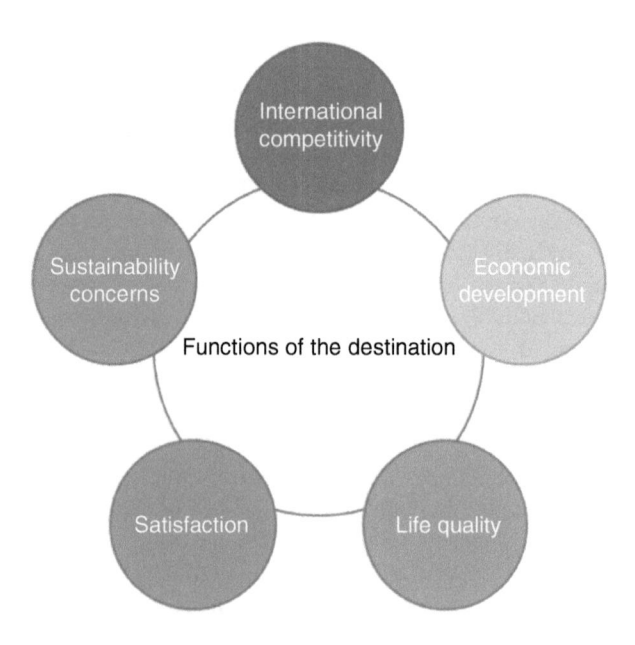

**Fig. 1** Functions of the tourism destination. Source: Adapted from Giménez (2006: 16–22)

## 2.1 The Role of ICT in the Tourism Destination Management

ICT can contribute to better manage and develop the space for the tourist experience both for the visitor and for the resident, with a view to contributing to innovation and entrepreneurship, associated with the sustainable tourist destination, which may arise through new products, new services or new tourist experiences (Ateljevic & Page, 2017).

Information and Communication plays an important role in a tourist experience, which can be supported by ICTs (Gretzel, Fesenmaier, & O'leary, 2006). ICT has contributed to transform consumer behaviour, since they are present in the three phases considered to carry out a tourist trip as showed in the Fig. 2.

The ICT can support the destination management in terms of sustainability and competitivity. As presented in the Fig. 2, they are the means par excellence to support the tourist in the phase of pre-consumption (before), consumption (during) and post-consumption (after) of a tourist product (Fotis, Buhalis, & Rossides, 2011).

In the pre-consumption phase, they are used to help plan the journey, to create a set of feelings that contribute to the expectation, and to acquire knowledge about the destination. At the same time, it helps in the process of becoming aware of the many options that meet the needs of the traveller, and consequently in the decision making, as well as provide mechanisms for carrying out service transactions and create an anticipation environment about the tourist experience (Gretzel et al., 2006; Narangajavana, Fiol, Tena, Artola, & García, 2017; Ukpabi & Karjaluoto, 2017).

In the consumption phase, in addition to the possibility of creating an ubiquitous connection, anywhere, anytime, through the mobile devices, they allow the navigation either in the space of the destination, through GPS, or through available information highways, through applications and portals, in order to obtain

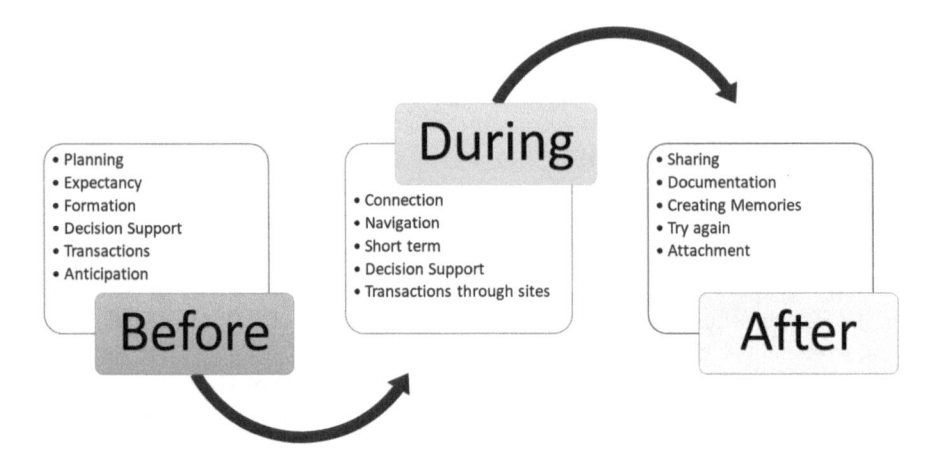

**Before**
- Planning
- Expectancy
- Formation
- Decision Support
- Transactions
- Anticipation

**During**
- Connection
- Navigation
- Short term
- Decision Support
- Transactions through sites

**After**
- Sharing
- Documentation
- Creating Memories
- Try again
- Attachment

**Fig. 2** Relation between the travel phases and the use of ICT. Source: Adapted from Gretzel et al. (2006)

information or through the purchase of complements to the tourist product, carrying out commercial transactions, through electronic stores (Gretzel et al., 2006).

In the after-consumption phase, the ICT allows the sharing of experience through the dissemination of memories built through feelings and documents produced during the trip, in a photographic or video format, which helps the tourist to feel the need to repeat the experience in the destination and thus contribute to its sustainability (Gretzel et al., 2006; Tung, Lin, Qiu Zhang, & Zhao, 2017).

The destination product is a set of dimensions, which includes the destination environment, service infrastructure and tourism destination experience (Murphy et al., 2000). The destination environment is the one that has the most impact and contributes to sustainable development, since it includes natural, political and legal, technological, economic, cultural and social factors, which conditionate the security, quality and development of the destination. It also serves as a basis for the development of the infrastructure associated with local and tourist services. The service infrastructure also causes impact on the destination and includes the support to the activity enrichment and the complementary product tourism, such as: shopping, recreation and attractions, food, travel, transportation, accommodation and auxiliary which increase the complexity, diversity, interest and wealth of the destination.

The tourism destination experience is the aspect that directly affects the tourist, while the destination environment is related to the destination, the experience is related to tourism, and the bridge between them is defined by the way the services were perceived, added value and how they contributed to the creation of affective memories, thus producing the tourist experience, as presented in the Fig. 3. In conclusion, the tourism destination experience can be seen as a result of the interactions between tourists and the tourist destination, taking into account several dimensions: sensorial, perceptual, social, affective and/or emotional (Tung et al., 2017; Tussyadiah & Zach, 2011) connected with the destination environment through the tourism services infrastructure.

## 2.2 The Influence of ICT in Tourism Experience

The conjugation between all the dimension of the tourism destination product and ICT can influence the tourism behaviour and their final tourism experience, as presented in the Fig. 4. When a tourist considers the use of technology in their tourist trip, this conjugation influences their behaviour, since it contributes to different activities associated with each phase of the trip (Dixit, 2016). For example, in the Before or planning phase, it helps to collect information on the destination, find more interesting places to visit, make hotel reservations taking into account the opinions of other travellers, look for information on public transport, the weather to decide what clothes to take, identify parties and festivals that will take place during the trip and helps the tourists choose and decide on what they will visit on the days they have to visit the destination. All these actions are carried out before traveling, although they are not concentrated only during this phase of pre-consuming. They also will take place in the next stage.

**Fig. 3** Conceptual model of the destination tourism product. Source: Adapted from Murphy et al. (2000: 46)

During the trip and with the support of technology, the tourist connects to the internet (Xiang, Wang, O'Leary, & Fesenmaier, 2015) and can search for information that complements the knowledge about points of interest that he has visited, searches for the most appropriate route according to his preferences to reach the next place he wants to visit, reviews of what he wants to visit or where he wants to stay, while he makes reservations for new travel supplements, searches for new services not identified in the previous phase and may even discover new interests and changes the travel plans that had initially defined. In addition, create memories in digital formats to produce a roadmap for his trip, which can be shared at that moment or in the future, in the next phase of his/her journey (Tung et al., 2017).

When the trip ends and they return home, in the after-sharing phase, tourists can share all the documents they have created on blogs, websites or in their profile on the social networks, while rating hotels and accommodation to help other travellers, creating digital memories which become available online for their own consumption, family, friends and other tourists (Tung et al., 2017).

The environment provided by technologies, both for the destination and for the tourist, has helped to develop mechanisms to support the competitiveness and sustainability of destinations, such as for the protection and dissemination of heritage (Unesco, 2017). Currently, the mechanisms include technology that involves the collection, exchange and processing of data, which have contributed to the development of intelligent destinations, business with intelligence and to the creation of intelligent experience (Gretzel et al., 2006). Associated with intelligent tourism, ICT has contributed to bridge the digital and physical environment using sensors and smartphones, technology that enables co-creation and collaboration between public and private companies.

**Before**
- Prepare the trip
- Collect destination information
- Discover more interesting places to visit
- Hotel reservations
- Search on public transport
- Search the weather
- Search for events
- Plan an itinerary

**During**
- Complement information already searched
- Through maps go through the paths to reach the desired places
- Get notifications from places closest to where you are
- Discover new products / events / sites
- Make reservations for events
- Search by services
- Check-ins

**After**
- Share comments, photos, and videos on social networks and personal blogs
- Evaluate hotels and restaurants
- Reply to comments
- Create and document trip memories to create your memories
- Relive the journey through your travel memories

**Fig. 4** Conceptual model of the destination tourism product. Source: Adapted from Buhalis and Amaranggana (2015)

## 2.3 The Potentialities of ICT to Customizing the Tourist Experience

The environment provided by current technologies associated with industry 4.0 (Lasi, Fettke, Kemper, Feld, & Hoffmann, 2014) and applied to the tourism sector, which include the use of smartphones, sensors, bigdata, private-public-consumer, virtual reality, cloud computing, and means to co-create experiences contribute to the mechanisms of collecting, exchanging and processing data automatically, which allow the creation of personalized experiences for the traveller (Höpken, Fuchs, & Lexhagen, 2018).

This technological environment, called smart tourism (Boes et al., 2015; Gretzel, Sigala, Xiang, & Koo, 2015), which includes the above identified technologies and involves the automatic processing of data, includes layers that contribute to: smart experience, intelligent business ecosystem and smart destination, with services based on the tourist location in order to create personal experiences.

The smart tourism destination environment enhancing tourism experience through tourist's expectation on personalized services, which can be associated to the three travel phases, in terms of transportation, accommodation, gastronomy, attractions and support services (Buhalis & Amaranggana, 2015).

In the "before phase", it is possible to customize services in terms of: transportation, such as plan itineraries, search schedules, recommend routes, save time in the reservation and purchase tickets; accommodation, hotel planning, room type, price choice, events nearby; time saving and personalized welcome message service; gastronomy, search for information on specific types of gastronomy, types and locations of restaurants; attractions, recommend attractions and provide information on attractions; and support services, where available, timetables and what services are available (Buhalis & Amaranggana, 2015).

Regarding of the "during phase", it is possible to customize services in terms of: (i) transportation, such as: real-time schedules, personalized transport, suggestion of alternatives; (ii) accommodation, welcome message, careful with customer preferences, adapted services; (iii) gastronomy, real time information taking into account preferences, social and physical context; (iv) attractions, co-creation through interactive maps, real-time information, information of the events near the place where you are; (v) and support services such as: how to get there, information about what is available, exchange of information in real time (Buhalis & Amaranggana, 2015).

In the last phase, or "after phase", it is also possible to customize services in terms of: (i) transport, such as: give feedback on services, receive promotions, support in looking for future places in transport; (ii) accommodation, feedback, receive promotional offers; (iii) gastronomy, feedback, receiving promotions, involvement in future actions/events of this nature; (iv) attractions, sharing, contributions to the experience and future memories, receiving offers and news; and (v) support services, monitoring the evolution of the service provided (Buhalis & Amaranggana, 2015).

In these context, smart tourism can be seen under three perspectives to take into account: (i) consumption, which refers to for example, the concern for personal information security, care about the actions of co-creation, psychological effects of ubiquitous use of technology, between others; (ii) services, in terms of the value of the information generated, the existence of adequate business models, the development of adequate collaboration mechanisms, among others; (iii) availability of technology, government of technological infrastructure, technological requirements, environmental and social costs (Buhalis & Amaranggana, 2015).

In view of the foregoing, the main objective of this study is to analyse the relevance of ICTs to improve the competitiveness and sustainability of the destination, in order to meet the needs of tourists.

## 2.4 The Research Questions

As was said before this research has as the main goal to analyse the relevance of ICTs to improve the competitiveness of the destination, in order to meet the needs of tourists by one side, and guarantee the sustainability, taking in consideration concerns about the life quality of their residents. So, in order to achieve it and considering the literature review presented, the research questions were defined bearing in mind the different phases of a trip: before, during and after. It is therefore intended to answer the following questions:

1. The use of ICT to search information on tourist destination?
2. Do you consider important and trustworthy to search information about a tourist destination on the internet?
3. Do you consider important to share information about a tourist destination through social networks?
4. What influence do the travellers comments shared on the social networks have on your choice of tourist destination?
5. Do you consider the use of mobile devices relevant during a trip?
6. What is the main action you take using ICT during a trip?
7. To share your trip, which social network do you use the most?

## 3 Methodology

After reviewing the literature and delimiting the research problem, a survey was prepared and published online in December 2017, consisting of 12 questions divided into 2 main groups: characterizing the sample and assessing the importance of ICT for the tourism experience associated to a travel. Two hundred and sixty-three (263) surveys were answered, however, only 242 were considered valid. The structure of the questionnaire allowed for the collection of the variables presented in the study.

After data collection, a descriptive statistics analysis was carried out to characterize the population, and statistical analysis using non-parametric tests was applied to the research questions.

Finally, the results were analysed and interpreted in order to obtain answers to the research questions.

## 4 Data Analysis and Research Results

### 4.1 Respondents' Profile

Data analysis and research results regarding demographic profile of the respondents, show that the majority are of Portuguese nationality (55%) and have between 25 and 50 years old (48%). The youngest group (under 25) represents approximately 38% of the sample. Respondents are primarily male (76%) and have an university or equivalent degree (80%), which indicates a high educational level in relation to the tourist demand in general. In the analysis of the variable related to the trip, the data show that the majority of visitors/tourists travel accompanied (87%), and the main reason for the visit is related to holidays (30%), followed by visits to family/relatives (48%).

### 4.2 Importance of ICT for the Tourism Experience Associated to a Travel

In order to analyse the research questions associated to the different phases of a trip: before, during and after—descriptive statistics and nonparametric tests uni and multivariate were used.

**RQ. 1. The Use of ICT to Search Information on Tourist Destination**
The use of ICT to evaluate alternative opportunities, compare and contrast offerings is perceived as being an important factor by a large proportion of the respondents. Table 1 shows that approximately 90% of the respondents always use ICT or use it many times to search information. Only a very small proportion use this tool occasionally. This finding is in line with previous studies, such as Xiang et al. (2015) who found that ICT is predominantly used during the before trip stage for information search purposes. Also, a study conducted by Sidali, Schulze, and Spiller (2009) to analyze the impact of reviews on the choice of holiday accommodation, found that more than 80% of users purchased accommodation recommended by reviews. This reflects an useful marketing tool for hotels and destinations.

**RQ. 2. Reliability of Information About Tourist Destinations in the Internet**
Respondents were questioned to express their perception about the reliability of information sources. Findings (Table 2) show that most of the respondents (47%) have reported to be neutral whereas 40% have affirmed they trust online information sources about tourist destination. On the other hand, the online information is not perceived as being very trustworthy source by 13% of the respondents. These

**Table 1** The use of ICT for searching information about tourist destination

| Variables | Frequency | Percentage |
|---|---|---|
| Occasionally | 7 | 2.9 |
| Neutral | 21 | 8.7 |
| Many times | 72 | 29.8 |
| Always | 142 | 58.7 |
| Total | 242 | 100.0 |

Source: Author's own table

**Table 2** Reliability of information online

| Variables | Frequency | Percentage |
|---|---|---|
| Disagree | 31 | 12.8 |
| Neutral | 114 | 47.1 |
| Agree | 85 | 35.1 |
| Totally agree | 12 | 5.0 |
| Total | 242 | 100.0 |

Source: Author's own table

findings might be explained by the particularities of the sample analysed, as older people tend to spend less time to grab information from internet (Lenhart, Purcell, Smith, & Zickuhr, 2010).

Continuing the analysis of this issue and considering the respondents' education level (Table 3) it was found that the confidence on online information decreases as a function of education level, as noted in Table 4 (statistical significance, $p = 0.011$). There are significant statistical differences between low levels and two other education level groups (degree and postgraduate), whereas the undergraduate respondents are more confident than those of higher degree. These findings are quite relevant signals for entities involved in the tourist phenomenon in order to strive for reliable content contributing to strengthening the trust of users.

### RQ. 3. Information Sharing Through Social Networks

Respondents were asked to express their willingness to share their personal data. As noted in Table 5, the majority of the respondents considers it very relevant or relevant (85%). These findings fully corroborate earlier study of mobile online networks of Xiang et al. (2015) which shows how social networks applications are being used to facilitate novel inter-tourist interactions in the physical world in real time.

Nationality proved to be a relevant variable when the information about tourist destinations promoted on social networks is considered ($p < 0.01$), assuming the Brazilian nationality individual higher importance compared to other nationalities. This result should be read in the light of the composition of the sample constituted mostly by individuals of Portuguese nationality, signalling that information in social networks about domestic tourist destinations is mainly relevant for foreign tourists.

**Table 3** Reliability of information and education level

| Education level | Number of respondents | Mean |
|---|---|---|
| Under degree | 49 | 143.62 |
| University degree | 120 | 120.37 |
| Postgraduate | 73 | 108.51 |
| Total | 242 | |

Source: Author's own table

**Table 4** Reliability of information and education level as grouping variable (Kruskal Wallis Test results)

| Chi-square | 8.996 |
|---|---|
| Gl | 2 |
| Significance Assint | 0.011 |

Source: Author's own table

**Table 5** Importance of sharing information through social networks

| Variables | Frequency | Percentage |
|---|---|---|
| Not relevant | 6 | 2.5 |
| Neutral | 31 | 12.8 |
| Relevant | 75 | 31 |
| Very relevant | 130 | 53.7 |
| Total | 242 | 100.0 |

Source: Author's own table

## RQ. 4. Influence of Travel Comments Shared on the Internet on Selection of Tourist Destination

The influence of online travel comments on destination choice is perceived as very relevant by approximately 75% of the respondents (Table 6). These findings are in line with previous studies i.e. Fotis et al. (2011) who found that 45% of prospective travellers checked social media websites when searching for destination and some 42% sought ideas on excursions and other leisure activities. This highlights the importance of online comments during the process of selecting a holiday destination, therefore it is a clear signal for the need to shape tourism products which can promote positive experiences for holiday makers and visitors as there is a great potential of sharing their experiences and influencing future travellers.

## RQ. 5. The Relevance of Mobile Devices During a Trip

Regarding the question, "Do you consider the use of mobile devices relevant during a trip?", results (Table 7) show the use of mobile devices are highly appreciated by these tourists, thus perceived as a relevant or very relevant tool during a trip. Going in depth on their perception of the relevance of mobile technologies and considering the respondents' age group of, it was found a significant statistical difference ($p < 0.05$) in assessing the relevance of mobile devices among all the age groups.

The age group average (25–49) assigns more significance, while the group 50 years old or more assigns less relevance. It was also found that the opinion about using mobile devices is influenced by respondent's education level, highlighting positively

**Table 6** Influence do the travel comments shared on the internet

| Variables | Frequency | Percentage |
|---|---|---|
| Never | 2 | 8 |
| Occasionally | 12 | 5 |
| Relevant | 186 | 57 |
| Very relevant | 42 | 17.4 |
| Total | 242 | 100.0 |

Source: Author's own table

**Table 7** Relevance of mobile devices during the trip

| Variables | Frequency | Percentage |
|---|---|---|
| Not relevant | 5 | 2.1 |
| Neutral | 27 | 11.2 |
| Relevant | 77 | 31.8 |
| Very relevant | 133 | 55.0 |
| Total | 242 | 100.0 |

Source: Author's own table

individuals with higher education level ($p < 0.016$). The group with the lowest education assigns less importance to the use of the smartphone. As in previous questions, these findings suggest that there may be an economic factor (hidden variable) associated to the group with lowest schooling level.

#### RQ. 6. Main Actions Using ICT During a Trip

As shown in Table 8 the majority of the respondents uses ICT to seek information on holiday destination and other places of interest (47%), followed by those who share photos, opinions and videos (29%). Thus, these findings corroborate previous questions analysis, where tourists, in general, use mobile technology for searching and sharing information and opinions on destinations and attractions.

#### RQ. 7. The Most Used Social Network to Share Trip Information

When it comes to social network to share trip experiences, as Table 9 shows respondents use various channels, with TripAdvisor being the most significant channel (58%), followed by Facebook, and Foursquare. Surprisingly only one individual of the sample mentioned booking.com. Overall, this seems to be in line with previous work such as, McCarthy, Stock, and Verma (2010), noting the use of different social platforms for different specific purposes.

## 5  Conclusions/Results

This study provides useful insights to tourism organizations managers and marketers for understanding traveller's use of ICT, highlights social media as a platform where travellers share their travel experiences and search for independent and trustful travel information. This may encourage tourism organizations managers to improve tourism product and its sustainability and marketers to recognize the need for developing

**Table 8** Main action using ICT during the trip

| Variables | Frequency | Percentage |
|---|---|---|
| Cancel or change bookings | 1 | 0.4 |
| Check-in, exchange of vouchers and other actions | 8 | 3.3 |
| Compare prices and or check the availability of accommodation | 15 | 6.2 |
| Communicate urgently with friends and/or relatives | 24 | 9.9 |
| View information about destination and/or places of interest | 114 | 47.1 |
| For reservations | 6 | 2.5 |
| Share photos, opinions and/or videos | 71 | 29.3 |
| Other actions | 3 | 1.2 |
| Total | 242 | 100.0 |

Source: Author's own table

**Table 9** Social network most used to share trip information

| Variables | Frequency | Percentage |
|---|---|---|
| Facebook | 38 | 15.7 |
| TripAdvisor | 141 | 58.3 |
| Google+ | 8 | 3.3 |
| Foursquare | 37 | 15.3 |
| Booking | 1 | 0.4 |
| Others | 17 | 7.0 |
| Total | 242 | 100.0 |

Source: Author's own table

effective communication strategies, particularly through social media, which enhances/create a strong destination brand image, and thus contributing to its competiveness.

This study shows that ICT are used during all stages of the holiday planning process (before, during and after holidays) however, to a different extent and for a different purpose.

From the results, it is evident that TripAdvisor is the most use channel of social media, (58%) followed by Facebook. Furthermore, this finding is a clear indication of the role of this channel in influencing destination selection.

Since TripAdvisor is the most important channel of social media used to share data, tourism organizations managers and marketers should pay close attention to reviews of their hotels and other institutional and economic players of the destination, respond to both negative and positive reviews. Travel providers and marketers might need to develop strategies to encourage travellers to create content, so that while creating their travel memories also become agents of the tourist destination.

Smartphones are perceived as relevant or very relevant tool during a trip by approximately 86% of the respondents. However, considering respondents schooling level, it was found a statistical significant difference between low schooling and higher-level groups (degree and postgraduate), suggesting that the undergraduate assigns less importance to the use of the smartphone.

The majority of the respondents considers sharing data through social networks relevant or very relevant (85%), suggesting as in previous studies, such as Xiang et al.

(2015) that social networks are new channels for novel inter-tourist interactions in the physical world in real time. However, the reliability of information available on social networks is perceived as being reliable by just over a third of the respondents, whereas 47% reported to be neutral about it. Considering the importance given to ICT as a mean of getting information on tourist destinations, this finding highlights the need for the entities involved in the tourism phenomenon to promote actions to strengthening user's confidence.

Tourism destination management entities should consider and ensure the existence of an excellent online reputation as well as the appropriate means for sharing information on the most appropriate and complete tourist information possible.

The major limitation of this study is the sample. The small size of the sample forces caution in interpreting the results and it blocks its generalization. Another limitations are related to the data collection period, which occurred along the Christmas holidays, limited the number of responses collected, and finally, the absence of potentially relevant variables, such as the level of income, which would make possible to draw more adequate conclusions and define strategic implications for the management of tourist destinations in a competitive and sustainable way.

**Acknowledgements** This paper is financed by National Funds provided by FCT—Foundation for Science and Technology through project CIEO (UID/SOC/04020/2019) and project CEFAGE (UID/ECO/04007/2019).

# References

Ateljevic, J., & Page, S. J. (2017). *Tourism and entrepreneurship*. London: Routledge.
Benckendorff, P. J., Xiang, Z., & Sheldon, P. J. (2019). *Tourism information technology*. Wallingford, UK: CABI.
Boes, K., Buhalis, D., & Inversini, A. (2015). Conceptualising smart tourism destination dimensions. In *Information and communication technologies in tourism 2015* (pp. 391–403). Cham: Springer.
Bornhorst, T., Ritchie, J. B., & Sheehan, L. (2010). Determinants of tourism success for DMOs and destinations: An empirical examination of stakeholders' perspectives. *Tourism Management, 31* (5), 572–589.
Buhalis, D., & Amaranggana, A. (2015). Smart tourism destinations enhancing tourism experience through personalisation of services. In *Information and communication technologies in tourism 2015* (pp. 377–389). Cham: Springer.
Chen, J. S. (2015). Tourism stakeholders attitudes toward sustainable development: A case in the Arctic. *Journal of Retailing and Consumer Services, 22*, 225–230.
Damayanti, M., Scott, N., & Ruhanen, L. (2017). Coopetitive behaviours in an informal tourism economy. *Annals of Tourism Research, 65*, 25–35.
Dixit, A. K. (2016). Enhancing tourism sector through the use of ICT. *Jagran Journal of Commerce and Economics*, 51–55.
Fotis, J., Buhalis, D., & Rossides, N. (2011). Social media impact on holiday travel planning: The case of the Russian and the FSU markets. *International Journal of Online Marketing, 1*(4), 1–19.
Fyall, A. (2011). Destination management: Challenges and opportunities. In Y. Wang & A. Pizam (Eds.), *Destination marketing and management: Theories and implications* (pp. 340–358). Wallingford: CABI.

Giménez, J. F. V. (2006). *Gestão integral de destinos turísticos sustentáveis*. FGV Editora.

Gössling, S., & Michael Hall, C. (2019). Sharing versus collaborative economy: How to align ICT developments and the SDGs in tourism? *Journal of Sustainable Tourism, 27*(1), 74–96.

Gretzel, U., Fesenmaier, D. R., & O'leary, J. T. (2006). The transformation of consumer behaviour. In *Tourism business frontiers* (pp. 31–40). London: Routledge.

Gretzel, U., Sigala, M., Xiang, Z., & Koo, C. (2015). Smart tourism: Foundations and developments. *Electronic Markets, 25*(3), 179–188.

Höpken, W., Fuchs, M., & Lexhagen, M. (2018). Big data analytics for tourism destinations. In *Encyclopedia of information science and technology* (4th ed., pp. 349–363). Pennsylvania: IGI Global.

Lasi, H., Fettke, P., Kemper, H. G., Feld, T., & Hoffmann, M. (2014). Industry 4.0. *Business & Information Systems Engineering, 6*(4), 239–242.

Lenhart, A., Purcell, K., Smith, A., & Zickuhr, K. (2010). *Social media & mobile internet use among teens and young adults*. Millennials, Pew Internet & American Life Project.

McCarthy, L., Stock, D., & Verma, R. (2010). How travellers use online and social media channels to make hotel-choice decision. *Cornell Hospitality Report, 10, 18*, 6–18.

Murphy, P., Pritchard, M. P., & Smith, B. (2000). The destination product and its impact on traveller perceptions. *Tourism Management, 21*(1), 43–52.

Narangajavana, Y., Fiol, L. J. C., Tena, M. Á. M., Artola, R. M. R., & García, J. S. (2017). The influence of social media in creating expectations: An empirical study for a tourist destination. *Annals of Tourism Research, 65*, 60–70.

Oliveira, E., & Panyik, E. (2015). Content, context and co-creation: Digital challenges in destination branding with references to Portugal as a tourist destination. *Journal of Vacation Marketing, 21*(1), 53–74.

Ritchie, J. B., & Crouch, G. I. (2003). *The competitive destination: A sustainable tourism perspective*. Wallingford: CABI.

Sidali, K. L., Schulze, H., & Spiller, A. (2009). The impact of online reviews on the choice of holiday accommodations. In W. Höpken, U. Gretzel, & R. Law (Eds.), *ICT in tourism 2009* (pp. 87–98). Dordrecht: Springer.

Tahayori, H., & Moharrer, M. (2006). E-tourism: The role of ICT in tourism industry, innovations and challenges. In *1st international conference on information and knowledge technology*, 1962.

Tung, V. W. S., Lin, P., Qiu Zhang, H., & Zhao, A. (2017). A framework of memory management and tourism experiences. *Journal of Travel & Tourism Marketing, 34*(7), 853–866.

Tussyadiah, I., & Zach, F. (2011, January). The influence of technology on geographic cognition and tourism experience. In *ENTER* (pp. 279–291).

Ukpabi, D. C., & Karjaluoto, H. (2017). Consumers' acceptance of information and communications technology in tourism: A review. *Telematics and Informatics, 34*(5), 618–644.

UNESCO. (2017). *Sustainable tourism and heritage*. Retrieved from https://www.youtube.com/watch?v=Hvv3lwngRP4&feature=youtu.be&utm_campaign=announcements&utm_content=8643&utm_medium=email&utm_source=platform

United Nations. (2019). *About the sustainable development goals*. United Nations. Retrieved from https://www.un.org/sustainabledevelopment/sustainable-development-goals/

Uysal, M., Sirgy, M. J., Woo, E., & Kim, H. L. (2016). Quality of life (QOL) and well-being research in tourism. *Tourism Management, 53*, 244–261.

Xiang, Z., & Gretzel, U. (2010). Role of social media in online travel information search. *Tourism Management, 31*(2), 179–188.

Xiang, Z., Wang, D., O'Leary, J. T., & Fesenmaier, D. R. (2015). Adapting the internet: Trends in travelers' use of the web for trip planning. *Journal of Travel Research, 54*(4), 511–527.

# Technology-Based Tourism Businesses: Extracting Actionable Knowledge and Insights from Social Networks

Jose Ramón-Saura, Pedro R. Palos-Sanchez, and María de la Cruz del Río-Rama

**Abstract** There are currently many technologies that are changing all types of professional ecosystems around the world. New technologies and business models based on the internet are producing the evolution of the tourism sector towards Digital Tourism, which uses innovation and the interconnection of products and services. The research aim of this study is to identify the main technologies and business models that are transforming the tourism sector into the new digital ecosystem. The trends that will influence the future of Digital Tourism can then be identified. To do this, an original approach is proposed, using textual analysis with data mining and visual data mining techniques with the User Generated Content (UGC) on the Twitter social network. The sample consisted of n = 25,434 tweets downloaded from the Twitter API with the hashtags #DigitalTourism and #Tourism. These were used to get insights and knowledge about the digital tourism industry using the technological innovations in the sector. The results of the research showed the main technologies and business models in the Digital Tourism sector, as well as the trends and future applications for the digital tourism sector. This research fills a gap in the existing research by using data mining techniques to obtain insights and knowledge from UGC about the Digital Tourism industry.

**Keywords** Digital tourism business · Technological-based strategies · Digital destinations · Business ecosystems

---

J. Ramón-Saura
Department of Business Economics, Rey Juan Carlos University, Madrid, Spain
e-mail: joseramon.saura@urjc.es

P. R. Palos-Sanchez
Department of Business Administration and Marketing, University of Sevilla, Sevilla, Spain
e-mail: ppalos@us.es

M. de la Cruz del Río-Rama (✉)
Department of Business Organization and Marketing, University of Vigo, Pontevedra, Spain
e-mail: delrio@uvigo.es

## 1 Introduction

There are currently many technologies that are changing all types of professional ecosystems around the world. New developments in information technologies, especially the Internet, have meant that many companies have adopted Internet-based business models and digital platforms with Internet users as the customers (Anttiroiko, Valkama, & Bailey, 2014; Atzori, Iera, & Morabito, 2010).

These new digital environments are ecosystems which use bi-directional information. Users have the power to publicly give their opinions and comments about the services and products to other users. Companies can also use these platforms to help their customers with any problems that may occur with their services or to inform customers about improvements to their products (Bakıcı, Almirall, & Wareham, 2013). These channels allow mass communication and promotions can be sent to themed user communities in only a few seconds.

These ecosystems provide and use improved channels for interconnectivity between companies and users. This has given rise to the appearance of new technology-based businesses in various sectors, such as tourism, finance, consulting, design, marketing, along with others (Sigala & Marinidis, 2012).

In this environment, companies use customer generated data on the internet to obtain information which allows them to create and improve competitive strategies and identify user patterns which allow them to provide added value to products and services. Various technologies have been created which provide companies with ways to collect data and transform unstructured databases into structured ones. Subsequent analysis of the databases allows knowledge, which was not available a few years ago, to be obtained with automated analysis processes (West & Gallagher, 2006).

New technologies such as big data, machine learning, artificial intelligence or data mining allow companies to apply new technological approaches and create new business models based on data and digital ecosystems. An important concept is Big Data, which is defined as information stored in enormous databases that cannot be managed with traditional software because of the size. Companies must use data analysis strategies from data science to obtain the data they are interested in (Bennett, Yábar, & Saura, 2017; Wang & Xiang, 2012).

One technique that has been used in the tourism sector is content analysis, in which companies analyze the content of a large amount of user generated data with qualitative software. Textual analysis is a strategy that allows companies to analyze the lexicon that is contained in these large databases in order to obtain keywords and key indicators that indicate ways in which value can be added to the company's competitive strategy. Other techniques and approaches can be used with the data to obtain different insights from the information stored in the databases of the sample (Wang, Park, & Fesenmaier, 2012).

In the last decade, several authors have become interested studying the evolution of the tourism sector with the digital environment (Benyon, Quigley, O'Keefe, & Riva, 2014; Minghetti & Buhalis, 2010; Hojeghan & Esfangareh, 2011; Santos,

Azevedo, Patriarca, & Leitão, 2019). This research has shown that the tourism sector needs to understand how travelers feel during their trips in order to offer them unique experiences to increase user satisfaction and include the sustainability of tourism ecosystems in the company strategies.

The Digital Tourism environment is the tourism sector using the Internet, new technologies and digital ecosystems and has also been studied by different researchers (Pelet, Barton, & Chapuis, 2019; Pierdicca, Paolanti, & Frontoni, 2019; Neumann, 2019). Different methodological approaches in research have detected the shortcomings of the tourism sector in terms of adapting to the new products, services and technologies of the digital era.

The aim of this research into digital tourism is to identify the main technologies and business models that are transforming the tourism sector into a new digital ecosystem. The trends that will shape the future of digital tourism are also identified. An original approach using textual analysis of User Generated Content (UGC) was proposed. The content comes from the user reviews, opinions and publications on the Twitter social network. The sample consisted of n = 25,434 tweets downloaded from the Twitter API with the hashtags #DigitalTourism and #Tourism, which were used to gain insights and knowledge about the digital tourism industry. Trends and future applications in the tourism sector were found and the investigation which fills a gap in research by using data mining techniques to obtain UGC insights.

## 2 Literature Review

### 2.1 Digital Tourism and New Business Models Using Technology

Different researchers have taken an interest in the digital tourism sector using new technologies. Benyon et al. (2014) investigated how digital tourism could create experiences for the user by comparing the tourists experiences when using traditional and digital tourism.

Minghetti and Buhalis (2010) researched the factors that facilitate the use of ICT by tourists when travelling and at their destinations by analyzing indicators in different cases. The importance of ICT in the tourism sector and in destinations, as well as the use of new technology in tourism business models was found. Kotler, Bowen, Makens, and Baloglu (2017) analyzed team and people management in the hotel industry, taking into account the importance of technological developments in tourism business models.

Hojeghan and Esfangareh (2011) studied the effects that new technologies in the digital economy have on the tourism industry. They gave examples of digital platforms that have business models based on the Internet and the interconnection with users. Tzanelli (2013) examined the effect of tourism on the evolution of cultural heritage management by using cinematographic interventions to document changes.

**Table 1** Previous research on technological based tourism businesses

| Author | Description |
|---|---|
| Maci (2013) | Investigate the evolution of communication in the tourism sector and how this has changed the sector |
| Munar, and Gyimóthy (2013) | Study the changes in tourism due to the use of "social media" |
| Baggio, and Del Chiappa (2014) | Evaluate the effects and extent of technological changes in the structure of the tourism system |
| Chiappa, and Baggio (2015) | Study how ICTs are used to exchange information and knowledge in the tourism sector |
| Saura, Palos-Sanchez, and Reyes-Menendez (2017) | Analyze mobile applications for tourism and the new business models which have appeared with them |
| Palos-Sanchez, Saura, Reyes-Menendez, and Esquivel (2018) | Analyze located-based applications in the tourism sector and the associated business models |

Source: Author's own table

The importance of technological developments in this scientific approach is emphasized in the study.

Benckendorff, Xiang, and Sheldon (2019a, 2019b) studied new technologies in the tourism system by using different approaches to promote good practices, case studies and examples that illustrate the evolution of the polyvalence of the tourism sector when adapting to new business models and emerging technologies. One example is the research presented by Dredge and Gyimóthy (2015) in which the collaborative economy in industrial tourism systems was analyzed and the technological evolutions that have been applied in this industry were described.

Table 1 shows the previous research on the topics of the present study.

## 2.2 User Generated Content (UGC) on Social Media in the Tourism Industry

The content generated by social media users is an area which has been studied on numerous occasions in the last decade. Van Dijck (2009) studied the content generated by users of the 2.0 web and social networks for tourism, finance, and consulting industries. The study is concerned with the 2.0 ecosystem in general, which was made up of web pages, social networks, wikis, blogs and other types of media and digital channels that allowed content to be shared bi-directionally.

Cha, Kwak, Rodriguez, Ahn, and Moon (2007) analyzed the impact of user generated content on the YouTube platform by studying the comments that users made about the content they watched. The comments about the content of the videos, the number of visualizations and the number of "likes" obtained were used to obtain insights and knowledge about successful content.

Daugherty, Eastin, and Bright (2008) studied the feelings shown in the UGC and the consumption that this produces. The feelings shown in the UGC of user profiles

**Table 2** Research on UGC in tourism

| Author | Description |
| --- | --- |
| O'Connor (2008) | Studied the communication between users on the Tripadvisor platform by analyzing the UGC about the reviews in order to make improvements for travelers at their destinations |
| Girardin, Calabrese, Dal Fiore, Ratti, and Blat (2008) | Studied the intentions and motivations of tourists from the positive content published in the UGC on tourism platforms |
| Cox, Burgess, Sellitto, and Buultjens (2009) | Research the influence of comments in UGC when travelers plan a trip and the effect it has on tourist at their destination |
| Reyes-Menendez, Saura, and Alvarez-Alonso (2018) | Studied the UGC on Twitter about the hashtag #WorldEnvironmentDay obtaining insights on tourism |
| Saura, Palos-Sanchez, and Rios Martin (2018) | Studied the user attitudes in the UGC about the hotels which won the TripAdvisor Travelers Choice Award 2018 |
| Saura, Reyes-Menendez, and Alvarez-Alonso (2018) | Analyze the UGC comments about the environmental management and sustainability of hotels on TripAdvisor and connect user behavior with the attitudes and feelings shared in the hotel reviews |

Source: Author's own table

was linked to the consumption of the digital content type. This research showed how feelings about the contents on a digital channel are an important factor in adding value to content on the Internet.

Krumm, Davies, and Narayanaswami (2008) analyzed six different articles on UGC about innovation. The different definitions of this type of content were studied with different approaches and perspectives. Future possibilities of study for these concepts on different platforms were also identified.

Smith, Fischer, and Yongjian (2012) compared the user generated content about different brand names on Twitter, Facebook and YouTube. The UGC from these platforms was studied to find the relationships that users have with the brand, as well as the types of comments made about favorite brands.

Thurman (2008) studied the UGC of its own users paying special attention to the "appearance of new journalists" who publish events in real time on social networks. This is known as "new journalism" or "journalism 4.0" in which users become journalists by sharing information as soon as an event occurs.

Dhar and Chang (2009) studied the UGC on digital platforms to obtain an estimate for the sales of music from the feelings expressed in the comments. UGC was found to influence the amount of music sold and future areas of study were planned (see Table 2).

Table 2 shows the studies in which insights are extracted from databases of UGC-type content on social networks.

## 3 Research Questions

In order to adapt the business models of the tourism sector to the demands of the market, CEOs and managers of hotels and companies must be aware of the technological advances available. In a digital ecosystem with an increasing number of technology-based business models, it is interesting to identify the trends that travelers will use in future strategies when organizing trips and when travelling.

With the current changes, technological advances and innovation in the tourism sector, business models must adapt to the demands of the market. In the current digital ecosystem, where large quantities of data are generated every day by users on the Internet, UGC has become an important tool to use when analyzing different industries in order to obtain insights and knowledge in a new way (Saura, Rodriguez Herráez, & Reyes-Menendez, 2019).

There are various platforms available to users where content can be published to express opinions and comment on different topics. Twitter, TripAdvisor or Booking.com have become suppliers of data for research to gain insights that help companies improve their business models and marketing strategies (Saura, Rodriguez Herráez, & Reyes-Menendez, 2019).

Therefore, this study aims to identify new technologies and business models which use innovation in the tourism industry by downloading UGC with the hashtags #DigitalTourism and #Tourism from the Twitter social network. The following Research Questions (RQ) were proposed in order to reach the planned objectives:

RQ1. What are the dominant themes of discussion in Digital Tourism and Technology-based Tourism Businesses?
RQ2. What network users and groups participate in these discussions about Digital Tourism and Technology-based Tourism Businesses?
RQ3. What are the new trends and future directions for Digital Tourism and Technology-based Tourism Businesses?

## 4 Methodology

Textual analysis with data mining techniques with posterior data visualization have been used in this research to identify patterns that help analyze insights and indicators for new technologies and business models in the digital tourism sector, These processes allow a holistic view of the knowledge to be obtained from the sample collected on Twitter.

The sample consisted of $n = 25,434$ tweets that were collected from the Twitter API from April 18 to April 25, 2019. Then a textual analysis of the UGC was carried out to obtain insights after applying different of data visualization and data mining techniques.

| Descriptive Analytics | Content Analytics | Network Analytics | Space-Time Analytics |
|---|---|---|---|
| Tweets Statistics | Sentiment Analysis | Reciprocity and Multiplexity | Time-Trend Analysis |
| Users Statistics | Polarity Analysis | Diameter, Bridge and Distance | Geo-Location Analysis |
| Engagement and Users Interactions | Emotion Analysis | Centrality and Cohesion | Period Series Analysis |
| Sentiment Reputation and Social Impact | Topic Modeling | Cluster and Clique Detection | Geo-Spatial Analysis |
| Words Cloud | Hashtag Analysis and Diversity | Homophily and Propinquity | Topic Density and Evolution |
| Hashtag Analytics | Lexical Diversity and Weight Percentage | Dimension and Community Detection | Topic Predictions |
| A. | B. | C. | D. |

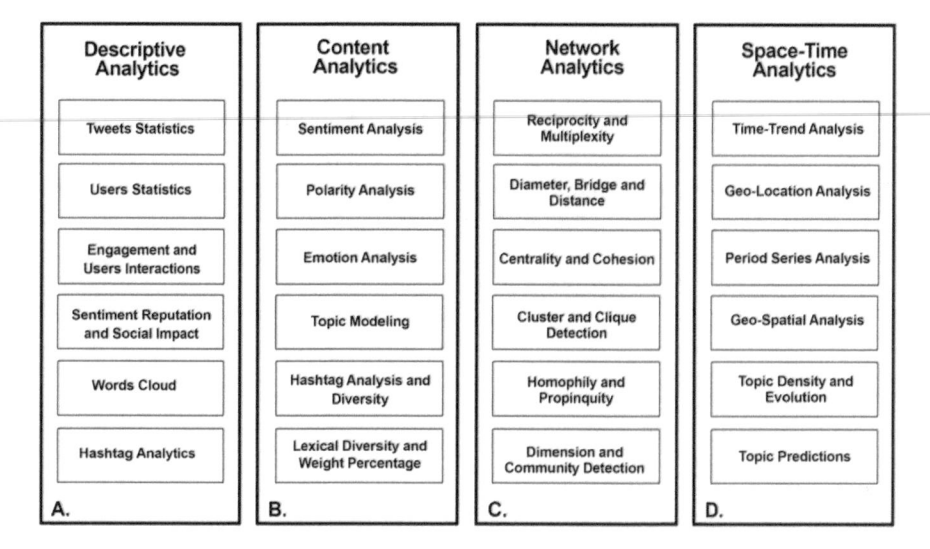

**Fig. 1** Main types of analysis in social media analytics. Source: The authors

Figure 1 shows the different methodological processes applied to data mining in order to obtain insights from samples collected from digital platforms and social networks (Aswani et al., 2018).

In this research a descriptive analysis is carried out with user account statistics, word-clouds and hashtag analytics. The content analysis used topic-modeling, hashtag analysis with lexical diversity and percentage weightings.

Network analytics techniques were chosen for analysis of dimension and community. The space-time analysis looked into topic density and evolution, as well as topic predictions.

The Nvivo Pro software was used for the textual analysis to find insights from the sample. This process uses a qualitative approach when analyzing data. There are many types of software available for textual analysis, along with algorithms written in Python and other programming languages (Saura, Rodriguez Herráez, & Reyes-Menendez, 2019).

The Nvivo software was used in this research because it has a simple interface that allows the researcher to easily and correctly classify and structure the database into nodes even though the researchers are not data experts. The data entry process is manual for Nvivo. The researchers created a structure of nodes for words identified as connectors, prepositions, articles, and plural forms. The following Eq. (1) was used to eliminate repeated words with the Nvivo software.

$$K = {k_i}/{n} \quad i = \{1,\ldots,n\} \quad n = \{1,x\} \tag{1}$$

An empirical approximation constant, which is called K, is established in Eq. (1). K is used to eliminate all words that are repeated in the different imported texts

(Saura, Palos-Sanchez, & Grilo, 2019). K is found from the query which searches the databases, so K is established for each sample or topic studied and is later compared with that found for rest of the samples. The global weight, Xs, is the average of K for all the identified topics or indicators (Saura, Reyes-Menendez, & Alvarez-Alonso, 2018).

The nodes are defined as data containers that can be grouped according to their characteristics. It should be noted that the design and development of nodes is a way to analyze pure data in order to achieve the highest possible quality from the descriptive research (Saura & Bennet, 2019). An important indicator when using this software is the weighted percentage (WP) which shows the number of times the data in a node is repeated in the sample. The following formula is used to calculate the weighted percentage:

$$K = \sum k_i/n_i = \{1,\ldots,n\} \; n = [1.25] \qquad (2)$$

As explained in the research by Saura and Bennett (2019), K is found from the query that is used to search the text. The behavior of each word and sample of text can be seen, and a value of K should be found for each research purpose. The average value of K for all the tweets was calculated in order to obtain the global value.

## 5 Analysis of Results

This study uses analytical techniques to extract actionable insights from UGC data on Twitter about the digital tourism industry. The following analysis was carried out for a total of 25.4341 tweets extracted from the Twitter API.

The descriptive statistics give an overview of the tweets, the users that interact with them and the engagement found (Bruns & Burgess, 2013; Saura & Bennet, 2019).

Of the total 25,434 tweets, 17,450 were original tweets and 7984 were re-tweets (RT). This indicates a very large amount of interaction between the parties involved with digital tourism on Twitter. A total of 5701 different hashtags were detected in the sample from 19,043 unique users who published UGC.

Over 58% of the tweets contained more than one hashtag, which indicates that many of the tweets were about several similar digital tourism topics. It seems that most of the users are active and visible on this social network, so the content used in this study is valid for obtaining relevant insights (Aswani et al., 2018).

A global vision was gained of the different community groups of the users in the sample after the textual analysis of the tweets. The algorithm for visualization and classification of data presented by Vincent et al. (2008) was used to detect the communities in the UGC (see Fig. 2) using the data visualization software, Gephi.

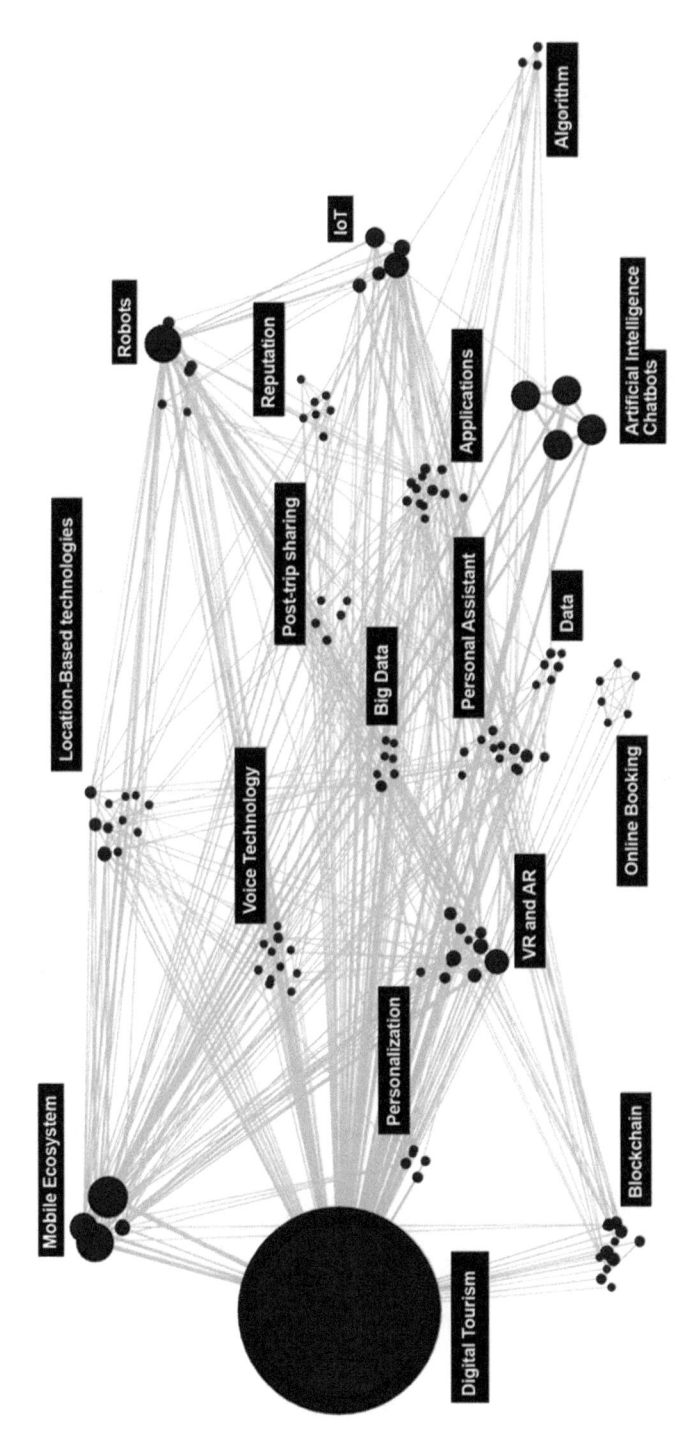

**Fig. 2** Main UGC topics for digital tourism on Twitter. Source: The authors

The modularity of the sample showed that the UGC and digital tourism users were grouped into communities.

The Lambiotte et al. (2009) algorithm was used to find the resolution of the results by grouping the results into communities of neurons or nodes. The modularity of communities is a measure of the network structure and was designed to measure the strength of the division of a network into clusters or communities (Vincent et al., 2008). Networks with high modularity have strong connections between the nodes contained in a module but weak connections between nodes in different modules. Modularity is often used in optimization methods for detecting community structures in networks and was also used in this way in this research.

Figure 2 shows the main UGC user communities found for the terms #Tourism and #DigitalTourism on Twitter by analyzing the neural connections and weights of the different nodes of the communities on the social network.

## *5.1 Technology Used in Digital Tourism*

The main technologies on which the digital tourism sector should be based in the near future are detailed below in order to create a roadmap for the future of the tourism sector using the technologies identified in this research and supporting the theoretical framework proposed by Little, Bec, Moyle, and Patterson (2019), Salerno (2019), Santos et al. (2019), Pelet et al. (2019), Bec et al. (2019) and Benckendorff et al. (2019a, 2019b).

### 5.1.1 Mobile Integration (Mobile-Friendly Ecosystem)

With the migration of the tourism industry towards a mobile-friendly ecosystem in which the smart-phone becomes the main tool used before, during and after trips, the integration of smart-phones into the tourism environment has become another necessary service.

Businesses must track the innovations in services and facilities using mobile technology such as Wi-Fi access or check-in using these mobile terminals.

Daily habits for tourists, such as ordering room service or opening room doors with the mobile smart-phone, are actions that show tourists that the facilities of hotels and tourist businesses are dynamic and mobile-friendly.

### 5.1.2 AI (Artificial Intelligence) and Chatbots

The use of Artificial intelligence has increased exponentially in the last few years. This is a technology that is being applied to chatbots and is increasingly being used to provide low cost services 24/7.

By correctly configuring and programming this technology and the services required, chatbots can offer information about schedules or tourist routes and offer additional applications that complement a hotels' or tourist business' services.

This technology can also be connected to other technological devices such as mobile smartphones so that assistants can analyze and decide on their own the best solution to a problem that guests, or travelers might have. These AI-based devices can resolve unforeseen events and provide differentiating value to the tourism business.

### 5.1.3 Integration of the IoT

As devices increasingly connect to the Internet and transmit data, the technology known as Internet of Things (IoT) gives meaning to the large amounts of data to enhance the travelers experience at the given destination.

These small devices can collect any type of information about the clients, from the time spent in a room, the temperature at which the guests feel comfortable or even their favorite water temperature.

The opportunities available when using IoT technology are endless when considering the volume of data collected and used.

### 5.1.4 Virtual Reality (VR)

Hotels, hospitality businesses, museums and other businesses in the tourism sector can implement this type of technology in their products and services. It is currently transforming various sectors such as video games, self-help and some health industries.

Virtual reality can provide the tourism sector with additional services that allow users to test an experience in advance or use a service provided by businesses in the tourism sector in a different way.

Technology which uses VR can provide travelers with additional services or innovative experiences at their destinations.

### 5.1.5 Virtual Personal Assistant

Personal assistants are being used more and more in the tourism sector. The developments in AI mean that more virtual personal assistants are appearing. These can help the traveler to prepare trips and make decisions about recreational visits during the trip.

Virtual assistants are being offered as additional packages by restaurants, hotels and hostelry services, which complement the sales and services offered by the companies in the tourism sector.

### 5.1.6 Augmented Reality (AR)

The use of AR technology in applications and mobile smart-phones allows travelers to enjoy innovative experiences. By using this type of technology, travelers and tourists can enjoy real-time recreations of historical monuments, old locations and other situations that are presented at the actual site in real time.

These AR applications are also being used as an additional service to attract customers as a complement to the normal tourist packages because they provide innovative activities and experiences with both visual and auditory content.

### 5.1.7 Robots

Robots are an innovative technology that is being used to provide services in the hotel and hostelry sectors. This technology uses machine-learning and artificial intelligence to offer physical assistants to accompany trolleys at check-in or check-out, or to provide room service orders and deliveries.

Several hotels and tourist accommodation offer advice from robots to answer questions or offer information about the tourist destination in any language. This technology will surely have an important role in the future of the tourism industry.

### 5.1.8 Block-Chain

The technology known as block-chains is changing organizations all over the world. This technology is usually associated with finance and accounting, but it can have an important impact on the tourism industry both digitally and offline.

Although there are not currently many examples of block-chain use in the tourism sector, this technology can be used in airports to identify and safely place passengers, review information and opinions, make reservations in tourist accommodation, as well as increase the security of online payments.

### 5.1.9 Location-Based Technologies

Smart devices that contain GPS have become an important tool when travelling around the world. Location-based applications not only have a GPS that helps travelers find their destinations, but also offer additional functions such as finding exclusive discounts and offering promotions depending on the location of the user.

Without a doubt, the application of location-based technology will help hotels to provide new products and increase the safety of trips and package tour.

### 5.1.10 Voice Technology and Apps

Voice technology and applications that use it have become a normal tool for tourists. Devices such as Google Home or Amazon Echo are voice aids that help users with their typical routine habits. Using these systems during trip can help travelers feel at home, which means that they can spend more time outside and, therefore, consume a larger number of products and services.

The complementary applications for this technology, known as voice-search, could be important in the future of the interaction between man and machine in the tourism sector.

## 5.2 Technology-Based Business Models in the Tourism Sector

From the results of this study and the research and results of Pelet et al. (2019), Pierdicca et al. (2019), Yuan, Tseng, and Ho (2019), Ankomah, and Larson (2019), Nam, Dutt, Chathoth, and Khan (2019), and Neumann (2019) the roadmap for business models using digital tourism are the following.

### 5.2.1 Focus on Data

As mentioned above, data is an important part of the new business ecosystem due to the amount of data that is generated daily. Companies such as Airbnb, Booking.com or TripAdivor are creating budget items for R&D&I projects to try to develop data-based improvements for their services.

There are different business models which exclusively use data for the tourism sector. The tourism sector generates data about the mobility of people, preferences for destinations and additional demographic and behavioral data.

The strategies of these business models are to sell data with reports that can detect patterns or market trends so that large tourism companies can use these types of insights to improve their service.

### 5.2.2 Digital Reputation Management

The fact that users can publicly share reviews on platforms such as Facebook, Twitter, Google Maps, Yelp or TripAdvisor has given rise to the emergence of new business models that use the digital reputation of companies operating in the tourism sector.

This business model is used in the tourism sector to purchase user reviews, which may be real or not, and to program bots posing as travelers to improve the scores of these businesses.

The users consult this type of platforms to make decision about their trips before making them, so a good digital reputation can influence users to decide to buy the tourist products or services offered.

### 5.2.3 Algorithm Use

There are business models that create algorithms that can be applied to the data collected by hotels, restaurants or even companies. These business models create algorithms technically, which is an expertise that tourism companies do not usually have, and later offer reports about the data found by applying these algorithms.

Tourism companies can use the results of these algorithms to improve their services, find trends and patterns in the complex data and consequently make their businesses profitable in the long term.

### 5.2.4 Big Data

The collection of data with IoT technology or with any other type of data collection technologies has given rise to the emergence of companies that sell the data collected in order to segment advertising on digital platforms in the tourism sector.

The objective is to make business more profitable by applying advertising segmentation strategies with big data type analysis.

### 5.2.5 Personalization

The personalization of products and services purchased by consumers in the tourism sector has become an important way to offer added value and innovation to the customer.

Personalization uses business models that offer exactly what the traveler wants with low-cost packages that connect flights and excursions through different countries with low-cost offers. There are also business models that specialize in luxury-based approaches and other types of personalization during the trip.

### 5.2.6 Online Booking Platforms

The use of the business model which works with online booking platforms is increasing strongly. There are many opportunities which include personalization of the service, but always using online booking platforms to find the supply and demand for solutions.

**Table 3** Summary of technologies and business model for digital tourism

| Digital tourism | Technology | Digital tourism | Main focus |
|---|---|---|---|
| Technology based | AI (Artificial Intelligence) and Chatbots | Business model based | Data |
| | Integration of the IoT | | Digital reputation management |
| | Virtual Reality (VR) | | Algorithms |
| | Virtual personal assistant | | Big Data |
| | Augmented Reality (AR) | | Personalization |
| | Robots | | Online booking platforms |
| | Block-chain | | Post-Trip |
| | Located-based technologies | | |
| | Voice technology and Apps | | |

Source: The authors

These platforms try to find the best deals in the sector by searching a multitude of different booking platforms and finally offer travelers the best results. In this way customers save time planning the trips. These business models usually receive income from advertising revenues or booking fees for the packages they offer.

### 5.2.7 Post-Trip: Sharing Is Living

There are also business models which take advantage of the importance of shared data and the attraction of UGC on social media and platforms by allowing travelers to post their experiences online. These business models use the content generated by travelers to show their travel experiences and also share the reviews made by other users.

Data is once again the focal point of profitability in this model, which relies on reports that add value and promote companies and destinations or give exclusive offers related to the shared data.

Table 3 shows a summary of the main technologies and business models for the future of the tourism sector.

## 6 Conclusions

This study has shown that the tourism and digital tourism sectors are influenced by technology and the evolution of the business models which are currently being used (Yoo, Sigala, & Gretzel, 2015).

In a sector which is influenced by data and consumption habits in a constantly changing digital ecosystem, the tourism industry is nowadays using the profitability of data and internet-based business models (Werthner et al., 2015).

RQ1 has therefore been verified from the main topics found in the data collected in the UGC on Twitter. The topics were identified by analysis of the hashtags used and the content shared by users.

RQ2 has also been identified and includes the network of users who share content on social media and platforms and who are important for the future of the tourism sector in the digital environment.

RQ3 used a textual analysis of the results from topics which were previously identified in order to find the future trends and directions of the digital tourism sector and the business models that it uses.

Two main lines of results have been obtained. Firstly, digital tourism which uses technology, and secondly, business models in the tourism sector that mainly use Internet elements, such as data, personalization, algorithms or online platforms, among others.

There is no doubt that CEOs and managers of hotels, restaurants and any other type of business in the tourism sector can use the results of this research to improve the added value they offer in their marketing strategies as well as using the identified elements to give additional value to their digital marketing strategies.

The application of data mining and data visualization research techniques can be of interest to other researchers who would like to apply this type of research methodology.

Researchers and academics can use the business models and technology found in the digital tourism sector for future research into tourism that can help to improve and consolidate marketing strategies and management on the Internet.

The limitations of the research are related to the size of the sample, the period of data collection, as well as the number of references consulted, and the number of topics and technologies analyzed.

## References

Ankomah, P., & Larson, T. (2019). Virtual tourism and its potential for tourism development in Sub-Saharan Africa. In *Advanced methodologies and technologies in digital marketing and entrepreneurship* (pp. 584–595). Pennsylvania: IGI Global.

Anttiroiko, A. V., Valkama, P., & Bailey, S. J. (2014). Smart cities in the new service economy: Building platforms for smart services. *AI and Society, 29*(3), 323–334.

Aswani, R., Kar, A. K., Ilavarasan, P. V., & Dwivedi, Y. K. (2018). Search engine marketing is not all gold: Insights from Twitter and SEOClerks. *International Journal of Information Management, 38*(1), 107–116.

Atzori, L., Iera, A., & Morabito, G. (2010). The internet of things: A survey. *Computer Networks, 54*(15), 2787–2805.

Baggio, R., & Del Chiappa, G. (2014). Real and virtual relationships in tourism digital ecosystems. *Information Technology & Tourism, 14*(1), 3–19.

Bakıcı, T., Almirall, E., & Wareham, J. (2013). A smart city initiative: The case of Barcelona. *Journal of the Knowledge Economy, 4*(2), 135–148.

Bec, A., Moyle, B., Timms, K., Schaffer, V., Skavronskaya, L., & Little, C. (2019). Management of immersive heritage tourism experience: A conceptual model. *Tourism Management, 72*, 117–120.

Benckendorff, P. J., Xiang, Z., & Sheldon, P. J. (2019a). *Tourism information technology*. Wallingford: CABI.

Benckendorff, P. J., Xiang, Z., & Sheldon, P. J. (2019b). The digital tourism landscape. In *Tourism information technology* (3rd ed., pp. 22–46). Wallingford: CABI.

Bennett, D., Yábar, D. P. B., & Saura, J. R. (2017). University incubators may be socially valuable, but how effective are they? A case study on business incubators at universities. In M. Peris-Ortiz, J. Gómez, J. Merigó-Lindahl, & C. Rueda-Armengot (Eds.), *Entrepreneurial universities: Innovation, technology, and knowledge management*. Cham: Springer. https://doi.org/10.1007/978-3-319-47949-1_11

Benyon, D., Quigley, A., O'Keefe, B., & Riva, G. (2014). Presence and digital tourism. *AI & Society, 29*(4), 521–529.

Bruns, A., & Burgess, J. E. (2013). Blog research: The 'computational turn' [Blogforschung: Der 'computational turn']. In *Historyblogosphere: Bloggen in den Geisteswissenschaften* (pp. 135–148). Munich: Oldenbourg Wissenschaftsverlag GmbH.

Cha, M., Kwak, H., Rodriguez, P., Ahn, Y. Y., & Moon, S. (2007, October). I tube, you tube, everybody tubes: Analyzing the world's largest user generated content video system. In *Proceedings of the 7th ACM SIGCOMM conference on internet measurement* (pp. 1–14). New York: ACM.

Cox, C., Burgess, S., Sellitto, C., & Buultjens, J. (2009). The role of user-generated content in tourists' travel planning behavior. *Journal of Hospitality Marketing & Management, 18*(8), 743–764.

Daugherty, T., Eastin, M. S., & Bright, L. (2008). Exploring consumer motivations for creating user-generated content. *Journal of Interactive Advertising, 8*(2), 16–25.

Del Chiappa, G., & Baggio, R. (2015). Knowledge transfer in smart tourism destinations: Analyzing the effects of a network structure. *Journal of Destination Marketing & Management, 4*(3), 145–150.

Dhar, V., & Chang, E. A. (2009). Does chatter matter? The impact of user-generated content on music sales. *Journal of Interactive Marketing, 23*(4), 300–307.

Dredge, D., & Gyimóthy, S. (2015). The collaborative economy and tourism: Critical perspectives, questionable claims and silenced voices. *Tourism Recreation Research, 40*(3), 286–302.

Girardin, F., Calabrese, F., Dal Fiore, F., Ratti, C., & Blat, J. (2008). Digital footprinting: Uncovering tourists with user-generated content. *IEEE Pervasive Computing, 7*(4), 36–43.

Hojeghan, S. B., & Esfangareh, A. N. (2011). Digital economy and tourism impacts influences and challenges. *Procedia-Social and Behavioral Sciences, 19*, 308–316.

Kotler, P., Bowen, J. T., Makens, J., & Baloglu, S. (2017). *Marketing for hospitality and tourism*. Singapore: Pearson.

Krumm, J., Davies, N., & Narayanaswami, C. (2008). User-generated content. *IEEE Pervasive Computing, 7*(4), 10–11.

Lambiotte, R., Delvenne, J. C., & Barahona, M. (2009). Laplacian dynamics and multiscale modular structure in networks. *Physics and Society*, arXiv:0812.1770v3.

Little, C., Bec, A., Moyle, B. D., & Patterson, D. (2019). Innovative methods for heritage tourism experiences: Creating windows into the past. *Journal of Heritage Tourism*, 1–13.

Maci, S. M. (2013). *Tourism discourse: Professional, promotional and digital voices* (Vol. 11). Genova: ECIG.

Minghetti, V., & Buhalis, D. (2010). Digital divide in tourism. *Journal of Travel Research, 49*(3), 267–281.

Munar, A. M., & Gyimóthy, S. (2013). Critical digital tourism studies. In *Tourism social media: Transformations in identity, community and culture* (pp. 245–262). Bingley: Emerald Group.

Nam, K., Dutt, C. S., Chathoth, P., & Khan, M. S. (2019). Blockchain technology for smart city and smart tourism: Latest trends and challenges. *Asia Pacific Journal of Tourism Research, 24*(5), 1–15.

Neumann, P. W. (2019). SESSION 3.2: Sustainable management of backcountry environments: Tourism, technology and climate change.

O'Connor, P. (2008). User-generated content and travel: A case study on Tripadvisor.com. *Information and communication technologies in tourism 2008*, 47–58.

Palos-Sanchez, P., Saura, J. R., Reyes-Menendez, A., & Esquivel, I. V. (2018). Users acceptance of location-based marketing apps in tourism sector: An exploratory analysis. *Journal of Spatial and Organizational Dynamics, 6*(3), 258–270.

Pelet, J. É., Barton, M., & Chapuis, C. (2019). Towards the implementation of digital through Wifi and IoT in wine tourism: Perspectives from professionals of wine and tourism. In *Management and marketing of wine tourism business* (pp. 207–236). Cham: Palgrave Macmillan.

Pierdicca, R., Paolanti, M., & Frontoni, E. (2019). eTourism: ICT and its role for tourism management. *Journal of Hospitality and Tourism Technology, 10*(1), 90–106.

Reyes-Menendez, A., Saura, J. R., & Alvarez-Alonso, C. (2018). Understanding #WorldEnvironmentDay user opinions in Twitter: A topic-based sentiment analysis approach. *International Journal of Environmental Research and Public Health, 15*(11), 2537. https://doi.org/10.3390/ijerph15112537

Salerno, R. (2019). Digital technologies for "minor" cultural landscapes knowledge: Sharing values in heritage and tourism perspective. In *Geospatial intelligence: Concepts, methodologies, tools, and applications* (pp. 1645–1670). Pennsylvania: IGI Global.

Santos, J., Azevedo, L., Patriarca, J., & Leitão, L. (2019). *Volunteered geographical information and digital social networks applied to tourism dynamics in the "Alta and University of Coimbra"*. UNESCO World Heritage Site.

Saura, J. R., & Bennet, D. (2019). A three-stage methodological process of data text mining: A UGC business intelligence analysis. *Symmetry-Basel, 11*(4), 519. https://doi.org/10.13140/RG.2.2.11093.06880

Saura, J. R., Palos-Sanchez, P. R., & Grilo, A. (2019). Detecting indicators for startup business success: Sentiment analysis using text data mining. *Sustainability, 15*(3), 553. https://doi.org/10.3390/ijerph15030553

Saura, J. R., Palos-Sanchez, P., & Reyes-Menendez, A. (2017). Marketing a través de Aplicaciones Móviles de Turismo (M-Tourism). Un estudio exploratorio. *International Journal of World of Tourism, 4*(8), 45–56.

Saura, J. R., Palos-Sanchez, P. R., & Rios Martin, M. A. (2018). Attitudes to environmental factors in the tourism sector expressed in online comments: An exploratory study. *International Journal of Environmental Research and Public Health, 15*(3), 553. https://doi.org/10.3390/ijerph15030553

Saura, J. R., Reyes-Menendez, A., & Alvarez-Alonso, C. (2018). Do online comments affect environmental management? Identifying factors related to environmental management and sustainability of hotels. *Sustainability, in Special Issue e-Business, 10*(9), 3016. https://doi.org/10.3390/su10093016

Saura, J. R., Rodriguez Herráez, B., & Reyes-Menendez, A. (2019). Comparing a traditional approach for financial brand communication analysis with a big data analytics technique. *IEEE Access, 7*(1). https://doi.org/10.1109/ACCESS.2019.2905301

Sigala, M., & Marinidis, D. (2012). Web map services in tourism: A framework exploring the organisational transformations and implications on business operations and models. *International Journal of Business Information Systems, 9*(4), 415–434.

Smith, A. N., Fischer, E., & Yongjian, C. (2012). How does brand-related user-generated content differ across YouTube, Facebook, and Twitter? *Journal of Interactive Marketing, 26*(2), 102–113.

Thurman, N. (2008). Forums for citizen journalists? Adoption of user generated content initiatives by online news media. *New Media & Society, 10*(1), 139–157.

Tzanelli, R. (2013). *Heritage in the digital era: Cinematic tourism and the activist cause*. London: Routledge.

Van Dijck, J. (2009). Users like you? Theorizing agency in user-generated content. *Media, Culture & Society, 31*(1), 41–58.

Vincent, P., Larochelle, H., Bengio, Y., & Manzagol, P. A. (2008, July). Extracting and composing robust features with denoising autoencoders. In *Proceedings of the 25th international conference on machine learning* (pp. 1096–1103). New York: ACM.

Wang, D., Park, S., & Fesenmaier, D. (2012). The role of smartphones in mediating the tourism experience. *Journal of Travel Research, 51*(4), 371–387.

Wang, D., & Xiang, Z. (2012). The new landscape of travel: A comprehensive analysis of smartphone apps. In M. Fuchs, F. Ricci, & L. Cantoni (Eds.), *Information and communication technologies in tourism 2012* (pp. 308–319). Wien: Springer.

Werthner, H., Alzua-Sorzabal, A., Cantoni, L., Dickinger, A., Gretzel, U., Jannach, D., et al. (2015). Future research issues in IT and tourism. *Information Technology and Tourism, 15*(1), 1–15. https://doi.org/10.1007/s40558-014-0021-9

West, J., & Gallagher, S. (2006). Challenges of open innovation: The paradox of firm investment in open source software. *R&D Management, 36*(3), 319–331.

Yoo, K.-H., Sigala, M., & Gretzel, U. (2015). Exploring TripAdvisor. In R. Egger, I. Gula, & D. Walcher (Eds.), *Open tourism – open innovation, crowdsourcing and collaborative consumption challenging the tourism industry*. Heidelberg: Springer.

Yuan, Y., Tseng, Y. H., & Ho, C. I. (2019). Tourism information technology research trends: 1990-2016. *Tourism Review, 74*(1), 5–19.

# Digital Accessibility on Institutional Websites of Portuguese Tourism

**Fátima Matos Silva and Isabel Borges**

**Abstract** In this chapter we address the problem of accessibility and accessible tourism concerning the various types of information and communication, namely, the digital information resulting from technological innovation implemented in recent years in various websites.

As we have been developing studies on the impacts of accessibility and accessible tourism, we consider it fundamental to analyse the compliance of Portuguese institutional sites in the tourism area with the new European directives and Portuguese legislation.

In this sense, the main objective of this chapter is to understand how the institutional Web content related to Portuguese tourism meets the accessibility requirements of the *Web Content Accessibility Guidelines 2.0* (WCAG 2.0), of the *World Wide Web Consortium* (W3C). The sample reflects the Portuguese panorama of institutional websites related to Portuguese tourism activity and promotion.

---

F. M. Silva (✉)
Department of Tourism, Heritage and Culture, Universidade Portucalense Infante D. Henrique, Porto, Portugal

REMIT – Research on Economics, Management and Information Technologies, Portucalense University, Porto, Portugal

CITCEM – Centre for Transdisciplinary Research Culture, Space and Memory, Research Centre (uID 04059), Faculdade de Letras da Universidade do Porto-FLUP, Oporto University, Porto, Portugal
e-mail: mfms@upt.pt

I. Borges
Department of Tourism, Heritage and Culture, Universidade Portucalense Infante D. Henrique, Porto, Portugal

REMIT – Research on Economics, Management and Information Technologies, Portucalense University, Porto, Portugal

CEGOT – Centre of Studies on Geography and Spatial Planning, University of Coimbra, Coimbra, Portugal

CEPESE – Centre for Studies of Population, Economy and Society, Porto, Portugal
e-mail: iborges@upt.pt

Overall, with respect to accessibility practices, it is possible to conclude that none of the websites analysed meets the compliance levels of WCAG 2.0. The results point to an inequality in the dynamics and development of the Portuguese territory.

**Keywords** Digital accessibility · Accessible tourism · Institutional websites · Portuguese tourism

## 1 Introduction

The Word Wide Web offers a vast amount of information and services, with the aim of improving people's lives, raising the quality of information accessed, without constraints of access to their content.

The information accessibility essentially refers to the right to access a series of virtual information, eliminating barriers in access to communication, ensuring the compatibility of equipment and programs, with content adjusted and presented in compatible formats, if possible, with all types of limitations. It is, therefore, extremely important to analyse and evaluate this issue, associated with the design and availability of the most varied information on web pages.

Recently, the European Community published, on March 21, 2019, new guidelines set out in the *European Accessibility and Standard Design for All Act*. Likewise, Portugal, in anticipation, published in October 19, 2018, Decree-Law n° 83/2018 on *Accessibility of mobile websites and applications*.

As we have been developing studies on the impacts of accessibility and accessible tourism (Silva & Borges, 2018, 2019a, 2019b) we consider fundamental to analyse, in a constructive perspective, the conformity of Portuguese institutional websites in the tourism field with the new European directives and the Portuguese legislation.

In this way, we intend to contribute to the awareness of the problems that the generality of the users of the websites related to Portuguese tourism have, and particularly those that, for various permanent or occasional disabilities, still see this difficulty increased by the small existence of accessible websites.

The main objective of this research work is to analyse how the institutional web content of tourism in Portugal meets the accessibility requirements indicated in the WCAG 2.0 (*Web Content Accessibility Guidelines 2.0*), of the *World Wide Web Consortium* (W3C).

The sample studied is based on 19 institutional web sites related to Portuguese tourism activity and promotion and reflects the Portuguese panorama.

Of course, the computer analysis of web site results does not move us. Rather, we want to obtain quantifiable data that can enhance the qualitative analysis of strengths and weaknesses. Based on these data, we intend to reflect on the needs of improvements that the websites studied require, from the perspective of the user, the tourist who has permanently or temporarily, limitations.

Thus, in methodological terms, we made a collection and, later, a critical review of the existing literature and its contextualization, regarding the referred themes.

Subsequently, we preceded to the survey of the representative sites, collecting the URLs; we collect the statistical data of the software; and, finally, we did the synthetic analysis of the data obtained.

In order to verify compliance with the recommendations of WCAG 2.0, whose Portuguese version was published in 2014 and developed by the Access Unit of the Foundation for Science and Technology, we use the automatic validator *AccessMonitor* for version 2.0.

## 2 The User with Special Needs

The term accessibility, in the context of the Internet, is related to the availability of information to all users, regardless of their limitations, technology or platform used. In the past, when referring to accessibility issues, we only thought about alternative versions of websites, that would allow reading for people with visual impairments. Nowadays, it is a question of allowing all users to access, in a perspective of apprehending, understanding, navigating and interacting with the Web, regardless of their particularities (visual, auditory, physical, speech, cognitive, neurological disabilities or elderly).

There is also another problem, as most people, including web designers, are not informed about accessibility issues.

There are currently several recommendations that must be followed by everyone to have access to the content. Among them we highlight:

- Recommendations for WCAG 1.0 (*Web Content Accessibility Guidelines*), used for several years;
- Recommendations for WCAG 2.0 (*Web Content Accessibility Guidelines*), published in 2008, which replace those previously mentioned, and;
- Recommendations WAI-ARIA 1.0 for *Rich Internet Applications*, published in 2017, and used to improve the accessibility and interoperability of web content and applications;

In the case of Portugal, it is important to consult the AMA—Agency for Administrative Modernization (http://www.acessibilidade.gov.pt) and the Access Unit of the Foundation for Science and Technology, which developed the tool *AccesMonitor*—WCAG 2.0 (http://www.acessibilidade.gov.pt/accessmonitor/).

For the authors Darcy and Dickson (2009, p. 34), "Accessible tourism allows people with specific mobility, vision, hearing and cognitive needs to travel in the most autonomous, independent way, on an equal basis with other tourists and with dignity, through the availability of products, services and tourism environments of universal design. This definition covers all people, including those who travel with young children, strollers, the disabled and the elderly." Although often considered a niche market, it is effectively growing. The World Health Organization estimates that about 15% of the world's population lives with some kind of disability.

Adapted technology can be a crucial tool in order to make the choice of destination and the travel possible for a person with special needs, even helping to reduce their own limitations, temporary or permanent. This type of segment must feel prepared to travel, having a real notion of the selection parameters of destination and what will they find when staying in the territory.

## 3 Motivations, Accessibility and Destinations

The decision-making process of a visitor with temporary or permanent special needs is decisive, which is why the economic agents of the destination should pay special attention.

The motivations that lead the tourist to travel, the barriers that he encounters throughout the decision-making process, as well as the various physical and/or intellectual impediments, must be analysed, studied and accessible solutions must be created.

Motivation is only one of the factors that can contribute to understand tourist behaviour, but it is a crucial variable, because it is the driving force behind all behaviour (Crompton, 1979; Fodness, 1994). Regardless of the greater or lesser degree of incapacity, the tourist always implies a motivation, or a set of motivations, that seduce them to go to the destination and to want to feel an integral part of it (Fontes & Monteiro, 2009).

The decision to travel, for visitors with special needs, is different from those that do not need the usufruct of special access conditions (Devile, Kastenholz, & Santiago, 2010).

They usually do not travel alone, and their relationship groups will tend to choose destinations where their needs are met, with as much autonomy as possible. Thus, the products offered by the territory supply should be more careful, always considering the diversification of demand needs.

More than a matter of physical access, accessibility in tourism is related to the environment, positive experiences, and gradual progression, until the potential demand of tourists with reduced mobility becomes in an effective demand (Yau, McKercher, & Packer, 2004).

Currently, access to information is an indispensable factor in the choice of tourist destinations. The main sources of value and competitiveness, in almost all sectors of economic activity, are based on image, brand, brand management and its form of promotion (offline and online). However, the various actors and the capacity for innovation, or knowledge and relationships with consumers, cannot be ignored. In fact, increasingly requires the ability to management, integration and cooperation capacity in a value-added network, targeted to the satisfaction of the consumer.

According to Buhalis (2000), tourist destinations compete mainly through image, as long as the tourist's image of destinations before the visit is a determining element in the purchase decision. A deficient lack of answers in tourism, to this segment that, temporarily or permanently, feels the need for development and knowledge, starts from the difficulty of the barriers found in the moment of choosing the destination, aggravating when the real obstacles to the usufruct of the tourist activity are verified.

The accessible tourism segment, a social phenomenon in growth that has very particular characteristics, should allow tourists with special needs to enjoy tourism products/services that in the past were unattainable. In fact, accessibility implies the possibility of access to public and private buildings, but also to transport and information and communication technologies (Buhalis, Eichhorn, Michopoulou, & Miller, 2005; Silva, Costa, & Macedo, 2009).

Given this scenario, the balanced development of a destination implies that all its components respond to the needs of tourist demand, as well as to its constant changes. Effectively, both the facilities and the services designed to meet the needs of tourists compete primarily through image and promotion—powerful means of attraction. Increasingly, we are looking for models for promoting and developing sites that are sustainable and that incorporate new approaches.

The strategic management of a destination should consider sustainable development, with a rational use of resources, the environment and the well-being of the communities, fundamental factors for future generations to enjoy conditions that are equivalent and/or better to those that exist currently (Saarinen, 2006).

The competitiveness of a tourism destination based on differentiation allows its positioning in the tourists' mind, based on the equality of the enjoyment of the tourist experience, to evolve in the path of sustainability.

## 4 Accessibility on the Internet: The Main Guidelines and European Legislation

In recent years, the European Union (EU) has developed a research and technological development work, where it addresses the needs and requirements of people with special needs. The promulgation of common European accessibility laws, conventions and protocols has also helped member states to adopt measures to safeguard the rights of the thousands of people with disabilities or with special temporary or permanent needs living in the European Union.

An important step was taken on 13 December 2006 with the signing of the United Nations Convention on the *Rights of Persons with Disabilities at United Nations Headquarters*, in New York, and entered into force on 3 May 2008. It should be noted that this document has obtained the largest number of signatories in the UN history for ratification of a Convention, being the first comprehensive human rights treaty of the twenty-first century.

With EU support, the ENAT—*European Network for Accessible Tourism*—was established in January 2006—a project-based initiative of nine sponsoring organizations in six Member States.

In 2013, the World Tourism Organization (UNWTO) issues several recommendations in the document *Accessible Tourism, Tourism for All*.

In 2015, prepared by the European Commission, the *Mapping and Performance Check of the Supply of Accessible Tourism Services* was published, which identified the tourism services that contribute to the Accessible Tourism market. In total, the study identified 313,286 providers with Accessible Tourism potential in EU Member States.

Most recently, the European Community made public, on 21 March 2019, new guidelines set out in the *European Standard Accessibility and Design for All Act*. The *European Standard EN 17161: 2019 Design for All—Accessibility following a Design for All approach in products, goods and services—Extending the range of users*, was published. The goal is to help organizations to develop a consistent approach by defining requirements that enable them to develop and deliver products, goods or services that can be accessed, understood, and used by all, including people with disabilities. As each user has their needs, characteristics or capabilities profile, it is crucial to take these factors into consideration when planning products or services.

This European standard defines the context requirements of the organization; the needs and expectations, ensuring the inclusion of people with disabilities; the integration of operational processes related to user requirements; leadership, policy and responsibilities to support a *Design for All* project, in order to ensure achievement of accessibility results; the design of the *Design for All* goals and how to achieve them; monitoring, among others.

The EN 17161 encourages organizations to take a consistent approach through a range of innovative and accessible applications, maximizing potential users of products and services, helping to increase the percentage of the population that can actively participate in society.

## 5 The Case of Portugal

The planning and strategic development of an accessible destination is primarily due to government agencies, an integral and crucial part of the tourism system. Through the implementation of laws, they force the stakeholders to create more positive and proactive responses and attitudes to the tourism offer. In fact, the Government, as a regulatory stakeholder, must play an active role in balancing the interests of the private and public sector, the local population and the visitors (Kastenholz, Eusébio, Figueiredo, & Lima, 2012).

Portugal has been, from the first moment, sensitive to issues related to accessibility on the Internet. It was, in fact, one of the first countries in the world to create legislation in this area. Despite the implementation of actions is not as fast as desirable, our country is referenced, in many studies and documents, as a pioneering and exemplary case.

In 1999, it was the first Member State to adhere to the accessibility guidelines of the World Wide Web Consortium (W3C).

The first initiative for the inclusion of accessibility was the promulgation of Decree-Law n°. 123/97, of May 22. This introduced technical standards, identified the elimination of urban and architectural barriers in public buildings, public facilities and public road. Subsequently, in 2006, this decree was revoked, and a new decree was promulgated, Decree-Law n°. 163/2006 of August 8, which is applied to the Government, local authorities, public associations, public institutes, public sector entities, among others.

By Resolution of the Assembly of the Republic (n°. 56/2009, of July 30 and n°. 57/2009), the *United Nations Convention on the Rights of Persons with Disabilities*, adopted in New York on March 30, 2007, is ratified, as well as its Optional Protocol.

In 2011, by Law n°. 36/2011, of June 21, Portugal defines for the first time the standards and digital formats to be adopted by the Public Administration. The following year, through the Resolution of the Council of Ministers no. 91/2012 of November 8, the Portuguese Public Administration would have to adopt the WCAG 2.0 Standards of the WC3 through the publication of the *National Digital Interoperability Regulation* (RNDI). Also, in that year, through two Resolutions of the Assembly of the Republic (131 and 132/2012, October), the Government of Portugal is recommended, for the first time, the creation of a strategy to promote accessible tourism in Portugal. Even in 2016 (Regulatory Order n°. 11/2016, of October 28), an *Accessible Tourism Support Line* was approved, which defined the conditions of potential applications.

With the introduction of the recent decree-law no. 83/2018 of 19 October, it is required that all websites comply with certain rules and implement them by September 2019. Portugal, therefore, transposes Directive (EU) 2016/2102 of the European Parliament and of the Council on the accessibility of websites and mobile applications, regardless the device used to access from public sector (except for public broadcasters).

The Article 4 defines the concept of accessibility: "the principles and techniques to be observed in the design, construction, maintenance and updating of websites and mobile applications in order to make their content more accessible to users, in particular, to people with disabilities".

It should be noted that the Decree-Law stipulates that the most accessible web sites and mobile applications must meet the requirements of perceivability (information and interface components), operability (to ensure that components and interface navigation are actionable), comprehensibility (easy to understand) and robustness (solid content interpreted in a reliable way). Entities should monitor using an automatic or semiautomatic validator, commonly used in the market, conduct usability tests with people with disabilities, making the results public.

One of the points mentioned are the Web Content Accessibilities, which allow it to be accessible to people with various types of disabilities, including blindness and low vision, deafness or hearing loss, disabilities in terms of cognitive limitations, movements limitations, speech disabilities and photosensitivity. It is also assumed that older people will have ease of use, of course, when the accessibility requirements are met.

The aim is to create websites that can be used equally by disabled and non-disabled users.

In detail, it is noted that the new *National Digital Interoperability Regulation* (RCM n°. 2/2018, of January 5) obliges public entities to use the Web accessibility content of the *International World Wide Web Consortium* (W3C), which developed the *Web Accessibility Initiative* program.

The public entities that are covered by this obligation are: the organs of sovereignty; central public administration services, including public institutes and decentralized state services; the regional public administration services; and, finally, the Government business sector.

These entities must comply with the compliance levels stipulated in Table III of RCM n°. 2/2018. In summary, it implies that all Internet sites that exclusively provide information and content are required to comply with level 'A' of WCAG 2.0 or ISO/IEC 40500: 2012.

As far as Internet sites that offer online services are concerned, the level to be achieved is the 'AA' level of WCAG 2.0 or ISO/IEC 40500: 2012, and the RNID regulation recommends that the level of accessibility should be 'AAA' for WCAG 2.0 or ISO/IEC 40500: 2012.

About 20 years later, Portugal has only 124 public administration sites accessible to people with disabilities. Of these, only three are fully accessible.

It should be noted that in the Tourism Strategy 2027, the theme of Accessibility is a priority, and *Turismo de Portugal* has developed various tools that aim to support entrepreneurs and managers of tourism destinations to make the national offer accessible. However, as we will see, several obstacles remain to be overcome in terms of websites.

## 6 The *AccessMonitor* Automatic Validator

The *Web Content Accessibility Guidelines* (WCAG) 2.0 cover a wide range of recommendations that aim to make website content more accessible to people with special needs.

Virtual accessibility is intended to cover a wide range of special needs, such as visual limitations (blindness and low vision), hearing impairments (deafness and low hearing), learning difficulties, cognitive and neurological limitations, such as those related to speech, language, physical and movement limitations, and photosensitivity.

If these guidelines are met, the content will be more accessible and easily usable, for a greater number of people with special needs and for the elderly individuals whose capacities change due to aging. They also often improve accessibility for general users. We must, however, be aware that, unfortunately, they do not address all the needs of people of all kinds, degrees, and combinations of special needs.

WCAG 2.0 was developed through the World Wide Web Consortium (W3C), in collaboration with people and organizations around the world, to provide common elements of Web content accessibility that can meet the international needs of people, organizations and governments at the international level. It is intended that they can be applied to the different existing Web technologies, now and in the future, and that can be verified through several automatic tests and several human validations.

In order to respond to the diverse needs of several stakeholders (programmers and Web designers, legislators, purchasers of goods and services, teachers and students), various levels of approach have been developed, including "global principles, guidelines general, testable success criteria, an abundant set of Sufficient and Counseling-type techniques, as well as documented common failures with examples, resource links, and source code availability" (https://www.w3.org/Translations/WCAG20-en-EN/).

As we have already mentioned, the four fundamental principles that constitute the foundation of Web accessibility are: perceptible, operable, understandable, and robust.

Based on these principles were created 12 guidelines that provide the basic goals to achieve to produce content more accessible to different types of users.

Although the guidelines are not stable, they are an important source of reference, as are the overall objectives, which help to understand the success criteria and improve the implementation of the techniques. As a result, success criteria were created for each guideline, which could be tested. In this way, it is possible that WCAG 2.0 will be used where requirements and compliance tests are required.

Based on the principles and criteria defined, three levels of compliance were created: "A" (the lowest), "AA" and "AAA" (the highest).

In order to prevent the success criteria that are not covered by the success criteria capable of being tested, informative techniques have been developed that fall into two categories: those that are of sufficient type to meet the success criteria and those that are advised type.

All these levels of approach (principles, guidelines, success criteria and techniques) have the ultimate and essential goal of providing guidelines to make content more accessible.

It should be noted that, even in the case of content that is at the highest level ("AAA"), it is not accessible to individuals of all types, grades or combinations of special needs, particularly in the areas of cognitive language and learning.

The program we use to know the accessibility of the websites we studied was *AccessMonitor* which is "an automatic validator that verifies the application of accessibility guidelines in the HTML contents of a website. *AccessMonitor* uses version 2.0 from the Web Content Accessibility Guidelines (WCAG 2.0) of the World Wide Web Consortium (W3C)" (http://www.acessibilidade.gov.pt/accessmonitor/nota_tecnica.html) that is available through the website of the Access Unit of the Agency for Administrative Modernization, IP (http://www.acessibilidade.gov.pt) and was the automatic validator for the WCAG developed by the *ACCESS Unit of FCT*—Foundation for Science and Technology, IP.

Currently there is a more up-to-date version of WCAG 2.1. However, there is no translation into Portuguese, so it does not allow validating the contents of the websites we analyse.

In order to be able to meet the compliance requirements, it is necessary to know which list of references to be considered.

We now need to briefly explain, based on the Quick Reference Guide to the requirements (success criteria) and techniques of the *Web Content Accessibility Guidelines 2.0* (https://www.w3.org/Translations/WCAG20-pt-PT/), which is considered essential for a website to be considered accessible.

It is extremely important that text alternatives are available to any non-text content, allowing adaptation to the needs of each user, such as extended print, Braille, read out loud (available as functionality), symbols and simpler language.

These contents must also be adaptable, but there should be no loss of information or structure. They must also be discernible, that is, the hearing and the visualization must be facilitated through the colour of audio elements, being always accessible through the keyboard.

Users should be given enough time to read and use the content. This text content must be readable and understandable.

All websites should provide help options when you enter the services, to avoid and correct errors, but also, this help must be available throughout the browsing and localization of content. So, they must be predictable.

It is also expected that the various support systems and technologies will be compatible over time.

Multimedia elements must provide alternatives dynamically or temporarily. That is, pre-recorded or live video or audio content must provide clearly identified text content, subtitles and audio description.

Lastly, content that, with the current knowledge of information technology, can cause epileptic seizures should not be made available.

As we refer, the program we use, *AccessMonitor* works fully on the web and automatically provides a qualitative report for each page submitted to it. This report is organized in two parts.

In the first part, a brief description of the collected sample and an exhaustive presentation of the compiled results are provided in two sections. The URL page is provided, a link to the page that was the subject of the analysis, and access to view the source code. It is also possible to consult the title of the page, the size in KB, the number of elements found and the date and time of the analysis. In the second part, the results are also divided into two parts, presenting the summary and the exhaustive detail of the tests performed.

In the summary, the *AccessMonitor* index is available as the "valuation unit used in all validator tests and the final result of which summarizes and quantifies the practices for accessibility expressed in WCAG 2.0" (www.acessibilidade.gov.pt/accessmonitor/).

The three types of results are stratified by three priority levels ('A', 'AA' and 'AAA').

*AccessMonitor* performs 86 tests, but only 78 enter into the quantitative index calculation, while the remaining eight contribute to the qualitative report, functioning as warnings, identified with a yellow triangle with an exclamation point in the middle.

The result of each test is presented by a green icon with a visa and the indication OK and those with an error are marked with that designation and a red circle with an X inside it.

Those who need more information about the detailed results should access the "linear version", where they will find various information about all the tests that have been carried out and various explanatory documentation and links to other documentation.

*AccessMonitor* displays the results (of a page or a sample of pages) in a scale of 1.0 to 10.0, thus, synthesizing in only one value the degree of satisfaction of the automatic tests performed by the validator.

In *AccessMonitor* there are four types of tests: true, false, decreasing and proportional. True type tests validate a given condition on a scale of 1–10 (very bad practice: 1, bad practice: 2 or 3, regular practice: 4 or 5, good practice: 6 or 7, very good practice: 8 or 9 and excellent practice: 10).

This program infers the degree of compliance with WCAG 2.0, and its analysis is transversal to the three priority levels. The current 86 *AccessMonitor* tests do not have a one-to-one correspondence with the 61 success criteria of WCAG 2.0 (that is, there is no one-to-one relationship). There are also success criteria that are impossible to analyse automatically and there are tests that apply to multiple success criteria.

## 7 The Digital Accessibility of the Analysed Websites

The sample chosen concerns, in most cases, the official websites of *Turismo de Portugal* and the Regional Tourism Entities (ERT), once these organizations are responsible for regional tourism development, in line with the national guidelines for tourism. Thus, the selected websites, out of a total of 19, were those of *Turismo do Porto and Norte de Portugal*, based in Viana do Castelo; Tourism of the Centre of Portugal, headquartered in Aveiro; the Regional Entity of Tourism of the Lisbon Region, based in Lisbon; the Tourism of Alentejo and Ribatejo, that is based in Beja and has two websites, one relating to the geographical area of Alentejo and another to Ribatejo; and the Algarve Tourist Region, headquartered in Faro.

Regarding the islands, these Regional Tourist Offices depend on the Regional Secretariats of the Azores and Madeira. Madeira is headquartered in Funchal and Azores in the city of Horta, on the island of Faial.

Also included in the study were the websites of the municipal entities of the largest Portuguese cities, such as Porto and Lisbon, and the websites made available to these cities by *Turismo de Portugal* itself.

Of course, the focus were the websites directly related to accessible tourism, such as the private non-profit Accessible Portugal, complemented by *TOUR4ALL* and the private *TOURISM FOR ALL*.

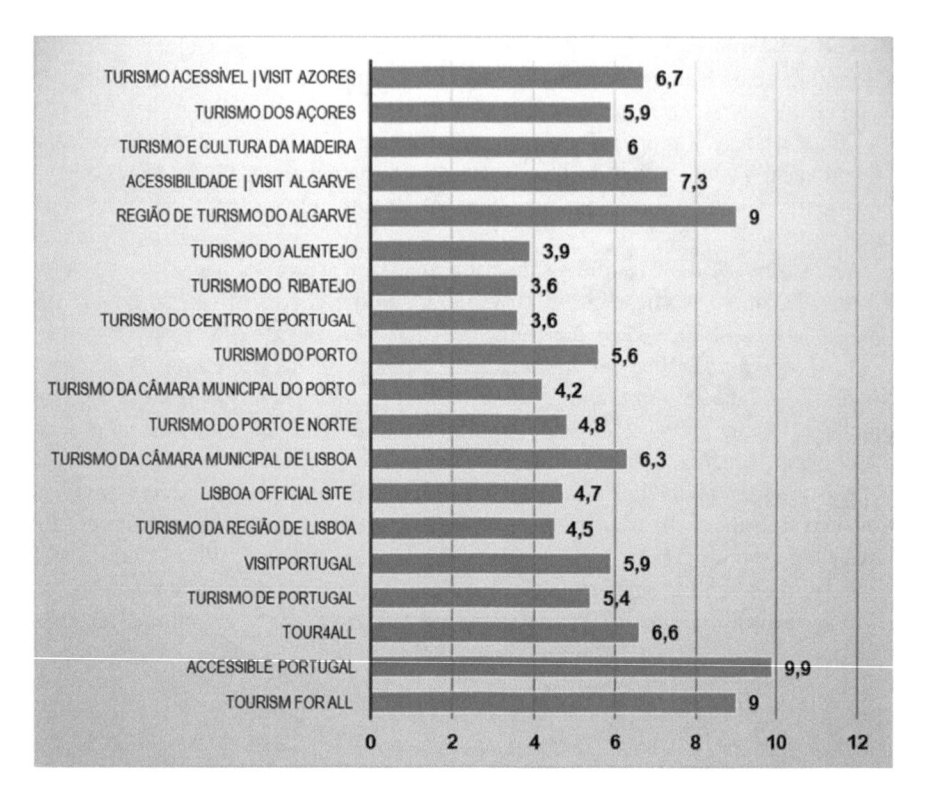

**Fig. 1** *AcessMonitor* indexes of the websites analysed. Source: Author's own figure

All the results of the analyses were compiled between March 26 and April 6, 2019. This data is important, since the websites are constantly updated, so the validity of analysis is relatively short.

The compliance of the analysed websites with the different levels is very variable (Fig. 1), although none reaches the desired value of 10 and very few approaches.

## 8 Quantitative Analysis

The quantitative analysis of the results has led to some conclusions on accessibility (Fig. 2). Unfortunately, as we have seen, the results denounce a still very weak accessibility for anyone other than a computer technician. Moreover, when the target audience of our study is the ordinary people, potential tourists, with or without special needs, but in many of the analysed websites will have several difficulties in finding and subsequently apprehending the information they need.

Of course, these difficulties are compounded when accessibility problems are of a physical nature.

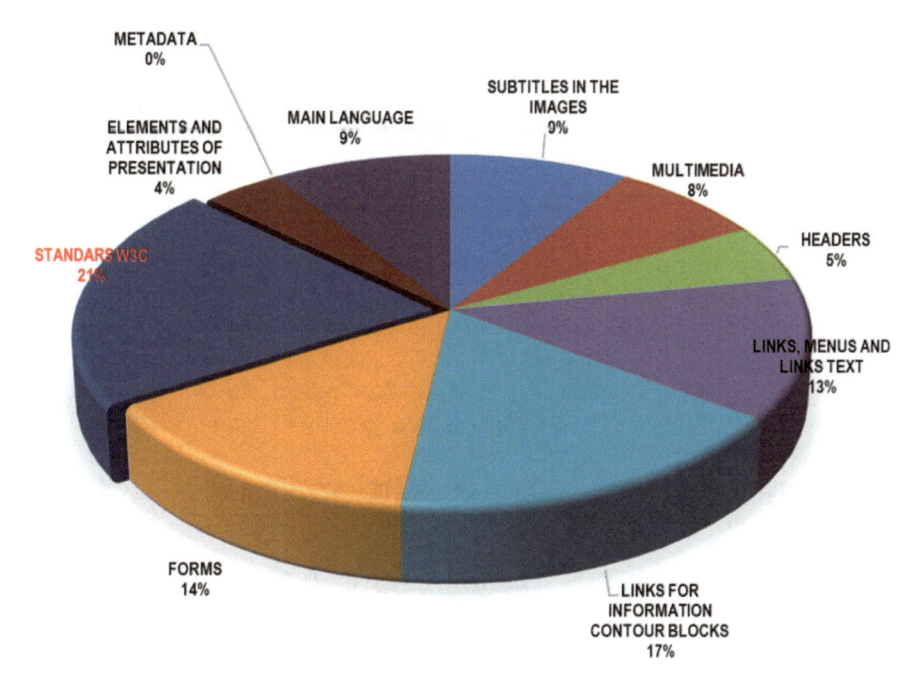

**Fig. 2** Percentage of level A errors presented in the websites analysed. Source: Author's own figure

We can thus verify that 10% of the website's present errors in the subtitling of the images, making it difficult to understand. In addition to these errors there are still some inaccuracies reported in the warnings. By principle, all images must have a subtitle, which does not happen.

Only one of the websites allows you to change the size of the letters, as well as to adapt the brightness. Also, what should not occur, is the existence of errors in the presentation of the main language, in the order of 10%.

The marking of headers presents errors in the order of 5%, which makes it difficult to understand, since the subjects treated are not "announced", being more difficult the search for the subjects and their subsequent reading, since in a great spot attention is lost.

As we can see from Fig. 2, 13% of the web sites do not show clearly the structure of the document, mixing styles, which also makes accessibility difficult. In terms of content presentation elements and attributes, errors are less significant, with a percentage of only 4%.

The largest number of errors occurs on websites that provide forms, which is 15% of the total. That is, information is not presented to contextualizes the subjects and to explain what should be filled. This creates a further obstacle, especially for people using assistive technologies, because they do not even have access to the explanation of what they must fill.

Other errors, in the order of 18%, are those in which links are presented to outline blocks of information, either by repeating often what has already been said or by being so extensive that users do not read them.

Websites with multimedia solutions present errors in 8% of cases, and there is no error in the metadata.

Most errors, 21% of the sample, are concentrated on the W3C standards—which, of course, leads to low compliance rates.

The analysis of the results of the "AA" and "AAA" level tests carried out presents fewer mistakes but a lot of warnings.

We find it tedious and unhelpful to re-enunciate all the percentages for which errors have been presented in relation to the "AA" and "AAA" level tests.

So, to sum up, we can mention that in terms of compliance tests at level "AA", the analysis of the 19 websites returned errors in a total of six errors concerning four websites.

Concerning the warnings, they are presented in relation to 15 Web sites, but in a rather high number of 36 alerts or calls for attention to possibilities for improvement—warnings.

Regarding the "AAA" level of compliance tests, which is considered to be the highest, the analysis of the 19 websites revealed errors in a total of 22 relating to 17 websites.

Regarding the warnings, these are presented in relation to 17 websites, numbering 23, concerning situations that may be subject to improvement.

All values here are revealing the problems that treated all web sites, although some more than others reveal, in terms of compliance with what is considered an accessible, all-purpose website. There is, therefore, a great path to be taken in terms of improvements.

## 9 Qualitative Analysis

Although the results may be acceptable at this time, because they are not yet ready to comply with the guidelines of the new legislation, they are surprising, given that they are the main means of dissemination and information of Portuguese tourism. The market niche for Accessible Tourism and its various valences does not yet deserve official attention.

Even in the situation of the two cases—Algarve Tourism Region, through the page Accessibility for People with Special Needs—Visit Algarve and the Regional Secretariat for Energy, Environment and Tourism of the Azores, through the page Accessible Tourism Visit Azores—, where the official websites already have pages built for people who have some kind of special needs, permanent or temporary, and which are the Portuguese showcase of accessible tourism, they have some errors.

It stands out for the positive, although it is expected, the scores of the websites Accessible Portugal and Tourism for All almost reaching the totality of the conformity.

Given that our goal is a qualitative analysis from the user/consumer perspective and it is practically impossible to present a study that involves the 61 success criteria that make up the WCAG 2.0, we will analyse only some of those that we consider more important for accessible tourism.

The elements chosen for the qualitative analysis were the captions of the images, the graphic buttons, the image maps, the multimedia use, the size of the letter, the forms, the menus, the headings and the indication of the main language. Also, here some of them are observed (Table 1).

We will begin to make an analysis of some of the best websites and, subsequently, a generalized one.

The company *TOURISMFORALL*, based in the Lisbon area, and member of *ENAT* (European Network for Accessible Tourism), explains on the homepage that intends to "Provide quality services to our clients, meeting their needs and expectations, regardless of their health condition, who wish traveling in or to Portugal, in comfort, safety, leisure, accessibility and continuity of their treatments to ensure their wellbeing".

This is an easy-to-use site that allows you to search. It is available in Portuguese, English, Spanish, French, German and Chinese. In some of the languages the information is not, however, complete. It also presents several brochures that can be downloaded in 19 languages on accessible tourism and shows almost complete compliance with the tests carried out, reaching the 9.0 index.

The private non-profit association *ACCESSIBLE PORTUGAL* was founded in 2006, also in Lisbon, and aims to promote Accessible Tourism for All in Portugal. It reaches the highest index of 9.9.

At the top of the page it allows you to quickly access the site map, which greatly facilitates access to, and is the only one of the 19 analysed which allows to increase or decrease the size of the letter and adjust the contrast, being essential elements to allow accessibility. It does not provide direct information in other languages or search possibilities for words. Also, it does not have the site symbol accessible.

This Association offers the *TOUR4ALL PORTUGAL* website (associated with *TOUR4ALL SPAIN*) and a mobile application APP *Tour4All*. Given that it is a page in permanent construction, its level of accessibility at the time of analysis was 6.6.

In these areas it is possible to access various information on accessible destinations, to look for accessible tourist resources and accessible experiences. You can also choose different activities in different countries, according to the accessibility criteria chosen by each user.

It has a simple and accessible language, allowing the insertion of new accessible tourism proposals, later validated regarding its degree of accessibility. It also provides information on various training actions.

The *TURISMO DE PORTUGAL* (Portugal Tourism) website, although it has a language and easy access, has a lot of information and many subjects, which makes it very complex.

It is only available in Portuguese and does not allow the search of subjects on the homepage.

In the site map you can more easily understand which areas and subjects can be found.

Table 1 Characterization of some elements of the websites analysed

| Websites home page | Accessmonitor index | Posting of accessibility symbol | Languages available | Photo subtitling | Research functionality | Reference to accessibility or accessible tourism |
|---|---|---|---|---|---|---|
| Tourism for all | 9.0 | No | 6 | Yes | Yes | Yes |
| Accessible Portugal | 9.9 | No | 1 | Yes | Yes | Yes |
| Tour4all | 6.6 | No | 1 | Yes | Yes | Yes |
| Turismo de Portugal | 5.4 | Yes | 1 | No | No | Yes |
| Visitportugal | 5.9 | No | 10 | Yes | Yes | Yes |
| Entidade Regional de Turismo da Região de Lisboa | 4.5 | No | 5 | No | Yes | No |
| Lisboa official site | 4.7 | No | 6 | No | Yes | No |
| Turismo da Câmara Municipal de Lisboa | 6.3 | No | 2 | Yes | Yes | No |
| Turismo do Porto e Norte de Portugal | 4.8 | No | 3 | No | Yes | No |
| Turismo da Câmara Municipal do Porto | 4.2 | No | 1 | Yes | Yes | No |
| Turismo do Porto | 5.6 | No | 10 | No | Yes | No |
| Turismo do Centro de Portugal | 3.6 | No | 4 | No | Yes | No |
| Turismo do Alentejo e do Ribatejo, E.R.T. (RIBATEJO) | 3.6 | No | 1 | No | Yes | No |
| Turismo do Alentejo e do Ribatejo, E.R.T. (ALENTEJO) | 3.9 | No | 5 | No | Yes | No |
| Região de Turismo do Algarve | 9.0 | No | 5 | Yes | Yes | Yes |
| Acessibilidade para Portadores de Necessidades Especiais\Visit Algarve | 7.3 | No | 5 | No | Yes | Yes |
| Secretaria Regional da Economia, Turismo e Cultura da Madeira | 6.0 | No | 5 | Yes | Yes | Yes |
| Secretaria Regional da Energia, Ambiente e Turismo dos Açores | 5.9 | No | 5 | Yes | Yes | Yes |
| Turismo Acessível\Visit Azores | 6.7 | No | 5 | No | No | Yes |

Source: Author's own table

It has an accessibility button explaining the criteria and the degree of compatibility, using the TAW 3 validation program, which allows it to be considered an accessible website. However, through the program we used it only reaches index 5.4.

It includes the *VISITPORTUGAL* website, which is already presented in ten languages. It has links to all the websites related to Portuguese tourism and its various regions, which we also study here. It has a page with some, but few, information aimed at accessible tourism (index of 4.6) such as: beaches, lodging and accessible transportation. It offers a video with Portuguese and English subtitles and audio description only in German.

The *REGIÃO DE TURISMO DO ALGARVE* (Algarve Tourist Region) is the institutional website that shows the highest compliance, presenting the 9.0 index. It also associates a page directed to the Users of Accessible Tourism, designated *Accessibility for People with Special Needs|Visit Algarve*, with an index of 7.3.

This promotional website of the Algarve makes explicit reference to the compliance with the accessibility guidelines for web content defined by the W3C. It indicates that the portal conforms to Level A of accessibility and has been certified through automatic assessments (TAW 3).

Although not achieving a substantial compliance index, the *SECRETARIA REGIONAL DA ENERGIA, AMBIENTE E TURISMO DOS AÇORES* (Regional Secretariat for Energy, Environment and Tourism of the Azores), (5.9) provides a page also directed to the needs of accessible tourism designated *Accessible Tourism| Visit Azores* (6.7).

We note from these entities a concern for this niche of tourism that, hopefully, will soon be able to count on improvements in the various Web sites so that they can be considered fully accessible.

All the other websites analysed present several errors and absences from fundamental criteria in order to be considered accessible. Many of them have no mention of this type of tourism (Table 1).

In the case of the two sites under the responsibility of City Halls, as confirmed by the *AcessMonitor* indexes, not being webpages geared to tourism, the information is not very accessible and clear. The concern of the Lisbon Municipality to provide an indication of the parking places for vehicles of disabled people is positive. In the case of Porto, there is a real-time chat available that can help answering questions. It also allows reading out loud texts relating, for example, to the city's heritage.

Some websites offer several brochures, with the possibility of being downloaded in several languages—for example, Porto and the Azores one. The latter has 20 brochures, being the one relative to the island of S. Miguel the most accessible.

The website of the Madeira archipelago also allows access to the island of Porto Santo website. It presents similar characteristics, but with a lower validation index (5.5) since it presents more errors (6), so we do not analyse it in detail.

Access is also available to the very recent website referring to the celebrations of the 600th anniversary of the Discovery of the Islands of Madeira and Porto Santo (discovered, respectively, in 1419 and 1418) which presents the index 5.0. This fact leads us to consider that the current website construction does not comply with the accessibility objectives and criteria that Portuguese law imposes.

Regarding the site of the Azores this is only one, although it provides diverse information on the nine islands of the archipelago.

Like other positive situations, in general terms, we can refer to the existence of the site map, which helps the search for information in situations where the website is not very intuitive.

As some negative points we can mention the occurrence, with some frequency, of the impossibility of an easier search, through search of words or concepts; some maps that do not exist or do not load; videos that, although advertised, do not exist or are not subtitled, nor do they allow the audio description; some photographs do not have subtitles, although we have, in general terms in the table presented, considered as having this functionality.

## 10 Final Reflections

The existence of international and national standards and their universal acceptance is a significant step on the road to a more accessible Internet.

This theme on the impacts of accessibility and accessible tourism, including all types of physical, informative, and communicational accessibility has been the object of several studies that we have undertaken (Silva & Borges, 2018, 2019a, 2019b) so we consider it fundamental to analyse the compliance of Portuguese institutional websites in the area of tourism, with the new European directives and with Portuguese legislation.

In this sense, the main objective of this chapter was to understand how the institutional Web content related to Portuguese tourism meets the accessibility requirements of the Web Content Accessibility Guidelines 2.0 (WCAG 2.0), of the World Wide Web Consortium (W3C).

Overall, regarding accessibility practices, it is possible to conclude that none of the analysed websites reaches the total level of conformity of WCAG 2.0 with the index 10.

The results point to an inequality in the dynamics and development of the Portuguese territory, at various levels, also with a substantial reflection in terms of informational, communicational and digital accessibility of different types of tourists.

Despite the substantial increase in solutions, the constant bet on digital innovation results have not reached the goals. We can say that to comply with decree-law n°. 83/2018, of October 19, which stipulates that all sites must comply with certain rules and implement them by September 2019, Portugal has a long way to go.

Living with a special need involves challenges but, on the other hand, it allows the possibility of unique experiences. The citizens access to these new potentialities of the Internet must be safeguarded and guaranteed. It is essential to provide equal access, equal opportunities to all, fighting all forms of info-exclusion.

A society of the knowledge age must trigger a change of mentalities where there is full participation, where the diversity of human and functional possibilities is respected and valued. An accessible Internet allows all people with or without special needs to participate more actively in society.

# References

AMA – Agência para a Modernização Administrativa. http://www.acessibilidade.gov.pt/
Buhalis, D. (2000). *Marketing the competitive destination of the future*. Tourism Management, 21 (1), 97–116.
Buhalis, D., Eichhorn, V., Michopoulou, E., & Miller, G. (2005). *Accessibility market and stakeholder analysis: One-stop-shop for accessible tourism in Europe (OSSATE)*. Surrey: University of Surrey.
Crompton, J. L. (1979). Motivations for pleasure vacations. *Annals of Tourism Research, VI*(4), 408–424.
Darcy, S., & Dickson, T. (2009). A whole-of-life approach to tourism: The case for accessible tourism experiences. *Journal of Hospitality and Tourism Management, 16*(1), 32–44.
Devile, E., Kastenholz, E., & Santiago, R. (2010). Inibidores à participação das pessoas com deficiência nas actividades turísticas. In N. Abranja, A. Marques, F. Coelhoso, & I. Carneiro (Eds.), *Turismo Acessível - Estudos e Experiências* (pp. 35–49). Mangualde: Edições Pedago.
Diretrizes de Acessibilidade para Conteúdo Web (WCAG) 2.0. https://www.w3.org/Translations/WCAG20-pt-PT/
Fodness, D. (1994). Measuring tourist motivation. *Annals of Tourism Research, 27*(3), 555–581.
Fontes, A., & Monteiro, I. (2009). O projecto "Louçã, Destino de Turismo Acessível": Um estudo de caso da aplicação de uma abordagem sistémica ao Turismo Acessível. *Revista Turismo & Desenvolvimento, 11*, 61–72.
Kastenholz, E., Eusébio, C., Figueiredo, E., & Lima, J. (2012). Accessibility as competitive advantage of a tourism destination: The case of Lousã. In K. F. Hyde, C. Ryan, & A. G. Woodside (Eds.), *Advances in culture, tourism and hospitality research* (Vol. 6, pp. 369–385). Bingley: Emerald Group.
Saarinen, J. (2006). Traditions of sustainability in tourism studies. *Annals of Tourism Research, 33* (4), 1121–1140.
Silva, M. F. M., & Borges, I. (2018). Religious tourism and pilgrimages in the central portuguese way to santiago and the issue of accessibility. In *Handbook of research on socio-economic impacts of religious tourism and pilgrimag* (pp. 375–395). Hershey, PA: IGI Global.
Silva, M. F. M., & Borges, I. (2019a). Accessible territories development: Hostels and religious architecture in Portuguese way to Santiago. In *Proceedings of the 2nd international conference on tourism research – ICTR 2019* (pp. 308–320). Academic Conferences and Publishing International, Reading.
Silva, M. F. M., & Borges, I. (2019b). Accessibility in the ways of Santiago: The Portuguese central way. *International Journal of Religious tourism and Pilgrimage, Ireland, 7*(2), 62–75.
Silva, A., Costa, M., & Macedo, M. (2009). Multiple views of sustainable urban mobility: The case of Brazil. *Transport Policy, 15*, 350–360.
Unidade ACESSO da FCT – Fundação para a Ciência e a Tecnologia. I.P. http://www.acessibilidade.gov.pt/accessmonitor/
Yau, M., McKercher, B., & Packer, T. (2004). Traveling with a disability: More than an access issue. *Annals of Tourism Research, 31*(4), 946–960.

# The Ethical Assumptions in Higher Education

Rui Pedro Lopes, Cristina Mesquita, Amador Durán-Sánchez, and Juan R. Coca

**Abstract** Higher Education Institutions (HEI) have been challenged to rethink their action and to adequate their mission to new contemporary realities. These challenges have been posed by the characteristics of democratic societies which led to the expansion of compulsory schooling, increased cultural, ethnical and gender diversity of students, and also the volatility, internationalization of labour market, and by the ephemerality of knowledge caused by accelerated scientific and technological development.

Considering this perspective, it is the responsibility of HEI to support the development of knowledge and skills that allows young people to make free and ethic choices, based on shared values, including respect and participation. Living in society, at the macro, meso or micro level, requires technical and scientific knowledge, enabling individuals to pursue a profession, contribute for their integration, independence and autonomy, and to contribute to the social and economic development. This requires complex competences that empowers them to take ethical decisions in their profession and in their lives, assume and share responsibilities, to respect diversity and differences of perspective, to negotiate, to build consensus and relations of reciprocity. HEIs should include these ethical assumptions in their actions and organizational practices, making visible the values of freedom, equality,

---

R. P. Lopes
Research Center on Digitalization and Intelligent Robotics, Instituto Politécnico de Bragança, Bragança, Portugal
e-mail: rlopes@ipb.pt

C. Mesquita
Research Center on Basic Education, Instituto Politécnico de Bragança, Bragança, Portugal
e-mail: cmmgp@ipb.pt

A. Durán-Sánchez (✉)
Economy Department, Faculty of Economics and Business, University of Extremadura, Badajoz, Spain

J. R. Coca
Faculty of Education of Soria, Department of Sociology and Social Work, University of Valladolid, Soria, Spain
e-mail: juan.coca@soc.uva.es

equity and solidarity. The incorporation of these ethical principles becomes more challenging at micro level, in the context of the classroom.

This chapter describes the ethical challenges that teacher/researcher faces during the teaching-learning process and his interaction with all the actors and how they can be applied in a teaching-learning activity. A case study is also presented, with two teachers and 40 students of an Informatics Engineering and 35 students of Basic Education programme. It highlights the importance of supporting pedagogical innovation in higher education, based on strong ethical foundations and on the development of collective learning goals and a shared vision.

**Keywords** Ethics · Teaching-learning · Social commitment · Higher education · Student's agency

## 1 Introduction

Within the mission of the HEI, and aware of the processes and the objectives, teachers have to be creative and sensitive in their practices, considering the interaction with the organization, the community and the students, ensuring their academic, social and ethical personal and professional development (Kemmis & McTaggart, 2005).

Ethical behaviours need to be stimulated during the teaching-learning process. This requires a change in the attitude of the teacher and also in the attitude of the students, with consequences for their professional and personal lives. This article describes the ethical assumptions in HEI and the ethical challenges that teachers face during the teaching-learning process and his interaction with all the actors and how they can be applied in a teaching-learning activity.

The development of an enabling environment, supported in democratic and participative principles, results in a community of learning. For that, it is necessary to develop teaching-learning strategies that help students understand the ethical assumptions implicit in the academic and professional life.

In this context, this study describes the teaching-learning process designed and developed by two teachers of two different higher education programmes. One in the degree on Basic Education, with 35 students and the other in the degree on Informatics Engineering, with 32 students. For this, the teachers developed strategies to allow students build awareness of who they are, what they know, the sense of belonging and becoming, and also the challenges that collaborative work bring in a learning community.

The case study shows that the learning process through the questioning, researching and dialogue has the potential to develop the sense of responsibility, the need to respect and be respected, the effort to discuss and get to the best collective decision (Flyvbjerg, 2002). Moreover, the evaluation of different moral standpoints, helps the students to adopt social and professional ethical behaviour.

Effective articulation, participation and responsibility sharing contributes to the development of the agency of the students. However, from the teachers' perspective, the implementation of the process is complex, requires time, effort and willingness to change.

## 2 Ethical Assumptions

The connection between the concepts of ethics and education is as deep as the relationship between *ethos*—the meaning of being human—and his self-fulfilment. Education is an area where the whole set of discourses, actions and strategies aim at the formation of man for a given society.

Ethics is understood as the study of human action, the accomplishment of the autonomy and freedom and the problematization of its moral subjectivity (MacIntyre, 2007). Education, the process by which a person becomes (and which involves the ontological dimension of the being and the epistemic dimension of knowing), should be configured in a pedagogy founded on the ethics of respect for dignity, which promotes the autonomy of the person in formation.

Education constitutes a mediating action between the subject, simultaneously complex and singular, and the reality that he experiences in each day. It is in this mediation that pedagogy was instituted as *phronesis*, usually translated as 'practical wisdom', sometimes as 'prudence', understood as the ability to think and act in relation to values, to deliberate about 'things that are good or bad for humans' [considering the Aristoteles definition, (Flyvbjerg, 2006)].

A person's action is developed in interaction with others, which highlights the moral assumptions related to his integration in the *polis*. There, the links between the microcosms of the *self* and the social macrocosms are established, and consequently the definition of regulatory mechanisms for such integration.

However, despite the issues involved in human interactions, ethical behaviour cannot be reduced to moral behaviours, considering that this retrenchment can lead the *self* to act from predetermined actions made by society, with no space for recreating himself. History has shown that the moral education conditioned human thought and action through a culture of ritualization, gesture and socialization that leads to the homogenization, contextualization and meta-projection of what is intended (Magalhães, 1999, p. 285).

On the contrary, we understand education as an emancipatory process that constitutes a space that enlarges, integrates and accepts man in the dimension of becoming and being able to transform, as proposed by Paulo Freire (1970). This perspective is based on a broader dimension of education, focused on interactional action, contextualized, renewed each day and sustained by ethical and humanizing principles. It is therefore, as stated by Dewey (1997) a century ago, rethinking education as a way of ethical reconstruction through Democracy. Whether it is through education that autonomy and freedom is achieved, school's role must support the students in their project to become enlightened citizens, participative, with agency and useful to the society through their specific actions.

This framework contradicts the technicist vision of the school, which forms a technical rationality that "transforms students into recipients, controlling the thinking and action that leads men and women to adjust to the world by inhibiting their creative power" (Freire, 1970).

As highlighted by Gambôa (2004)

> under the metaphor of 'growth' and the command of pragmatic reason, education is a process of conquest, a personal and social research / transformation where autonomy and citizenship are inseparable expressions of the same progressive (continuous and interactive) form of being: to be more, to grow, the path that leads morally to democracy (p. 11).

We understand, therefore, that regardless of the area, training in Higher Education must be understood in a praxiological dimension, whose ethics of relationships inform humanized action for the good of the professionals, organizations and societies where they are integrated. We assume a praxis-centred view of education, where theory and practice (or practice and theory) dialogue in a movement that favours the interpretation of experience which, in turn, leads to a better understanding of action and intentional modes of action, is based on a transformative pedagogy (Freire, 1970). A pedagogy that goes beyond the didactic, technicist or academicist vision of training (Houssaye, 2004, p. 10) to assert itself as a praxiology.

In this context, higher education organizations and particularly the classrooms where the pedagogical action takes place, and because there are students who are appropriating the specific knowledge about a particular profession, should be understood as professional learning communities.

In this sense, we understand a classroom as a social learning system because, like other social systems, it presents: (1) an emergent structure within which complex and dynamic relationships develop; (2) an organization of its own; (3) ongoing negotiations among members; (4) the shared perception of cultural and identity meanings.

The main idea recreated in this article is related to conceptualizations about the social nature of human learning, inspired by anthropology, social theory (Foucault, 1980; Giddens, 1986; Lave, 1988; Vygotsky, Cole, Cipolla Neto, Menna Barreto, & Afeche, 2008) and by the theory of systems, which places the learning perspective on the person's relations with the world, understanding that the "human being is to be a social person in a social world" (Wenger, 2010, p. 179).

Classrooms, as social structures, develop professional and social learning because the involvement of members in this social context is accomplished through a dual process of meaning development. On one hand, members participate in the life of the group directly, performing activities, talking and reflecting about the knowledge needed for the profession. On the other hand, within the community, physical and conceptual artefacts such as words, concepts, documents, methods, narratives and other forms of reification are produced that reflect the shared experience from which actions are organized.

Building meaningful learning, in a social context, requires participation and reification in an interconnected way, thus constituting an active, dynamic and living process of learning (Wenger, 2010).

This framework supports the study described in the following sections, which narrates the efforts of two teachers and their students in the construction of two learning communities, supported by the awareness of the singularity and the complexity of each element of the group, respect for cultural diversity, the importance of building a sense of group and the development of strategies that enhance the development of skills necessary to solve complex problems, think critically, be creative, demonstrate emotional intelligence, be able to judge and make decisions, work with others and adapt to new situations.

## 3 Methodology

The case study described in this chapter encompasses two classes from two different programmes, one in the Basic Education and another in Informatics Engineering. The values and ethical assumptions for each profession are dictated or specified by professional associations or orders. However, as stated above, as citizens of a democratic system, students should develop ethical awareness and democratic participation regardless of the profession and scientific area. Thus, among others, the responsibility of the higher education teacher also includes the stimulation of this awareness through the development of the teaching-learning process and the definition of adequate class environment based on these principles.

In this multi-context case study, the teacher starts by relinquishing his instituted power, opening the opportunity for the development of the students' agency (Pijano, Scott, & Knight, 2014). Students are included in all the aspects of the teaching and learning process, such as the design of the pedagogical methodologies, the definition of the content, and the pace to follow (Gülcan, 2015).

The methodology follows a descriptive and interpretative approach based on multiple data collection instruments and techniques, including class observations, field notes, students' written work, open question questionnaire and the individual portfolio. The approach starts by asking the students to formalize their (self-)learning contract, in which they describe their learning objectives and attitude (Table 1).

During the semester, students were stimulated to adopt a joint intellectual effort between colleagues and with the teacher, in a process of collaborative learning, with influence in the students' achievement, persistence, and attitudes about learning, contributing to equal participation by all members of the team, working with the others in a collaborative and friendly way, increased conceptual learning or increased engagement (Knoch, 2004). They work together in heterogeneous groups, assembled and organized through several group dynamics techniques, fostering their communication skills, inclusion awareness and commitment (Mesquita & Lopes, 2018). During the semester, students are required to prepare inter-group and

**Table 1** Collected data

| Material | Description | Timing |
|---|---|---|
| Learning contract | The self-learning contract, written by the student and presented to the class | Beginning of the semester |
| Group definition | Open-question questionnaire to assess the students' opinion about the importance of group definition strategies | Middle of the semester |
| Field notes | Teachers' written field notes | During the semester |
| Class observation | Class observation video and comments | Beginning, middle and end of the semester |

Source: Author's own table

in-group presentations, as well as written reports. This gives students the opportunity to assume an active role, through the strategies of questioning, researching and dialoguing, to develop the sense of responsibility, the need to respect and be respected, the effort to discuss and get to the best collective decision.

Teachers register field notes and commented observations of remarkable situation in the classroom (Lopes & Mesquita, 2016). Finally, at the end of the semester, a closed question questionnaire is distributed through the students to assess their satisfaction with the pedagogical methodology and the success on the teaching-learning process.

The qualitative approach was performed through content analysis, with data triangulation and cross-verification of the collected evidence of both contexts (students of Informatics Engineering and students of Basic Education). Content analysis allowed to create a category system that emerged from the collected data. Data will be presented based on the reflections, field notes collected by the teachers, coded with the letter R and FN respectively, followed by a number. Students were also represented by a capital S followed by a number.

The results are discussed in a narrative that emerges from the teaching-learning process developed in the two curricular units. This process was developed in order to promote students and teachers' ethical attitudes and the formation of the learning community from three strategies: (1) the establishment of learning contracts as an instrument to foster self-awareness about each member's singularity and complexity, and the diversity of the group. The objective of this strategy was the create an enabling environment, an atmosphere of openness, respect and empathy among all the participants; (2) different strategies of group formation, considering the necessary transformation of the group into a learning community. Two strategies were used for students to participate and develop a sense of belonging and sharing; (3) stimulate collaborative work and the development of necessary transversal skills considered relevant in social and professional experiences.

## 4 Results and Discussion

The results were discussed in light of the necessary ethical attitudes to build a learning community, such as: respect for students' diversity, assume equal opportunities for learning, involve the students in the learning process, develop creative classes, work cooperatively, communicate (teacher-student; student-student), negotiation and establishment of consensus.

The study was developed in the classroom, excluding online and e-learning scenarios. The experimental comparison was performed in the classes of Network and System Management (N = 32) and Didactics of the Knowledge of the World (N = 35).

### *4.1 Enabling the Environment: Creating an Atmosphere of Openness*

When students enrol a higher education programme, they follow some inner desire or conviction, usually associated to the possibility for a better life (Kelly et al., 2017). Regardless of their main motivation, what they are, the challenges they faced, the options they did, and all the previous academic, personal and professional experiences made the student what he/she is in the moment he/she starts studying at a high level. This starting point define the attitudes of the students towards the colleagues, the teacher and their own learning process. Their perception regarding the learning process, the professional requirements and the learning the procession process contributes to their ability to learn, to collaborate, to communicate as well as to their openness to develop moral attitudes towards the profession.

At the beginning of the courses mentioned in this study, students are requested to write a learning contract, in which they should provide answers and reflections about seven questions: where have I been? where am I now? where do I want to go? how do I get there? how will I know if I have arrived? how do I evaluate my learning? what measures do I need in order to assess myself?

The learning contracts were an important instrument for the awareness of all the elements of the group about the human condition. Students were invited to present their learning contract to the group, which allowed all to recognize a common humanity and, at the same time, the cultural diversity of the colleagues.

From the data analysis, of the text written and the observations performed by the teachers during the presentation, several aspects emerge. In this study, four categories were considered as fundamental: (1) the assumption of the human singularity; (2) the consciousness of the diversity; (3) the self in the professional option and (4) the necessary articulation between affection and rationality.

1. The assumption of the human singularity

   A relevant aspect that emerges from the data analysis is related to the importance that students, from both courses, to reveal their human condition, reflected in the narrative that details their personal and familiar paths that led them to the study degree and the institution. These narratives give relevance to their human and social frailties.

   > One of my goals is to be someone in life, to live my life the best way possible. And, perhaps, to return to my family everything they gave me, because without them it would not be possible for me to attend the degree I always wanted (S3, GSR).

   > A week before I knew I was coming to here, my father passed away. There were many doubts about coming, but it was the willpower that my father always had that kept me going and would not give up something that I always wanted because of his death, as he asked us so much (S9, LEB).

   ### Express the pride of the options and situations of their life

   > Almost finishing the degree, I can say for sure that I made the proper choice, I chose what I like, and I would do it again. The university path, although difficult, is worth it, this degree gave me, beyond practical and theoretical knowledge, an excellent thrust to the future (S1, GSR).

   ### Express their responsibilities in their options

   > It wasn't an easy decision, mainly because of economical reasons. I had to work and study and, in this led me to choose a technology degree, because it was available in my home town and I was able to harmonize both things (S2, GSR).

   Students were able to exteriorize their singularity, their life, giving to the colleagues and the teachers, in a selfless and generous way, all their intimacy, their complete and complex being that includes their mental, psychological, physical, affective, intellectual and subjective self.

   In this process, the teachers, in their double function as teacher and researcher, payed attention to the presentations, actively listening, respecting each student's time, inducing silence and questions, and supporting the class members in the development of mutual respect and in the development of empathy, necessary to the human experience, reflected in the academic and professional relations that each will have to assume. In this respect, some students refer:

   > I never thought that there were so difficult lives (...) the teacher knew how to give the necessary time and space for S10 to express, unquestioned, telling us with her gaze that our silence was the best way to support her (FN13, LEB).

   > I never imagined that in a higher education class I was given the opportunity to talk about what I am and what I intend to be. This work [learning contract] helped me to know my colleagues better, to understand that we all got here with different previous experiences. That it is necessary to respect the colleagues, because each one of them has important aspect in their life that made them what they are now (FN13, LEB).

2. the consciousness of the diversity

The understanding of the other implied, from the students, the awareness of the cultural diversity, the academic, the rhythms, paths, wills and expectations about the degree. The consciousness of the diversity is remarkable in some of the students' words:

> I was two and a half years with these colleagues and only now I was able to know something about them. It is so interesting to see where each of us came from. Now I understand better the situation of many of the colleagues (FN7, LEB).

> I am now aware that we don't think all the same way, but that each of these students is a person that needs to be respected, just like a child with whom we are going to work. To do a learning contract should be mandatory (FN5, LEB).

> Technical knowledge is not everything. For me, the true value of the degree is in keeping with the teachers and colleagues. Sharing knowledge is essential, as well as sharing real experiences with others. This is something that a self-taught cannot do (S2, GSR)

It seems to emerge, from the students' words, the awareness of the diversity if the group members, assuming a mean to develop tolerant relationships at the service of democracy. To assume democracy in the group supposes to feed on the diversity of opinions, both the for and against to rethink and rebuild their own ways to see the world, but also for the negotiations, the development of consensus and the free expression of ideas.

3. The self in the professional option

Most of the students reveal a positive image of the profession, assuming that their choice was not taken on impulse, but that it was supported by their connection to the degree. Their choices are often influenced by their representations about the profession that allow them to anticipate the pleasure it will provide them in the future.

> With 18 years old, the time for all decisions, to choose the degree that possibly would define my future could be the most difficult thing to do. It wasn't in my case. I always liked the technology and the potential of development and evolution, so engineering would be my starting point. Second, I was interested in manipulating and developing applications, websites, systems and other things. So, the idea of Informatics Engineering would be the most appropriate choice. In addition, the high rates of employability are also a fundamental factor for choosing this area (S4, GSR).

> If the aptitude that I think I have for the area of Education is confirmed on the exercise of the profession, I imagine myself to be a teacher in the initial years of schooling. Since I was a little girl, I built up the idea of what would it be to be a good teacher. (...) Being autonomous, being responsible and able to create positive, constructive and lasting interactions among all those involved in the educational process. Being able to do differently, to high scope, not to be attached to a physical space, bounded by the walls of a classroom (S11, LEB).

4. the necessary articulation between affection and rationality

The students were situated in the academic learning that they carried out until that moment. What seemed most obvious, became the most dubious. After all, what do I know about this curricular unit and what do I want to know? This was an issue that involved their reflection on the academic and professional knowledge essential to the exercise of the profession. They wrote what they knew, what they wanted to learn, and assumed that the unknown and the pleasure of learn more aroused their curiosity. They have revealed awareness that the teachers and the methodologies they use will be important for their involvement, for the construction of community-based learning to be shared and challenged.

> My knowledge about Network Systems is not enough, which is why I was curious. After a brief survey I learned that this area is increasingly playing a key role in information technology. In reality, this is a very demanding area from the technical point of view, largely because of the enormous range of technologies and services that the administrator must know in order to be able to ensure the correct functioning of a computer network (...). I have high expectations regarding the curricular unit because the teacher was able to arouse our interest with the challenges proposed, and with the interactivity of a "game" in which we will have to conquer our castles, after the teacher explained the motivation of the class in the overall was at its maximum (S1, GSR).

> Since my first enrollment in the LEB, the learning was not merely curricular. As we progress in the sequence of content, informal learning also stems from the interpersonal contact that naturally exists. In this concrete curricular unit, I know that it demands adequate curricular articulation and I know that the strategies that the teacher use lead us to participate, to open our minds and to reflect on what we are learning (S24, LEB).

Learning contracts allow students to situate themselves in the group, to understand that the construction of a community, where everyone felt they belonged, would imply respecting their diversity, providing equal opportunities for learning, getting involved in the learning process, communicate their learning processes, open their minds to build shared knowledge. The conditions were set for building a learning team. In the following section the process, the advantages and the difficulties of constructing a learning team are described, with students who are inhabited by an academic model of learning.

## *4.2 Group Formation Under Different Strategies*

Building a learning community on a praxiological approach requires the creation of conditions that promote the development of skills necessary to solve complex problems, think critically, be creative, demonstrate emotional intelligence, be able to judge and make decisions, work with others and adapt to new situations. To achieve these skills, it is necessary to introduce changes in the way students learn and, consequently, in the way teachers teach. In this context, the use of small groups has been increasingly prevalent to foster students' interactivity and problem-solving skills (Roschelle & Teasley, 1995; Stump, Hilpert, Husman, Chung, & Kim, 2011;

Van den Bossche, Gijselaers, Segers, & Kirschner, 2006). This presupposes that students are selected and integrated in specific teams, according to some group formation strategy.

There are several strategies for group formation. Broadly, the groups can be formed by the students, by the teacher or independently, with the help of automated tools or applications. Each approach has specificities that value some aspects and neglects others. For example, student selection groups can lead to less diverse teams and fail to integrate some students, leading to a feeling of being left and to reduce the potential contribution of the elements that were left out. Intentional teacher formation strategies require a good knowledge of the characteristics of all students and to have the sensitivity to the effects each has in a group. Finally, random assignment means that each student in the class has an equal likelihood of being selected into a group (Chapman, Meuter, Toy, & Wright, 2006; Maqtary, Mohsen, & Bechkoum, 2017).

As referred previously, a questionnaire was applied to assess the students' perceptions about group formation strategies. A total of 47 answers were received and considered valid, with 22 from Didactics of the Knowledge of the World and 25 from Network and System Management.

From the open-question data, the following analysis emerged:

1. Student-selected group formation

Students are unanimous in referring that they prefer this method of group formation. They believe that if they feel comfortable, they are more available to learn:

> Working in groups formed by students is always an advantage, because feeling comfortable is the best way to be "relaxed" in the learning process.

They clearly assume that they prefer choosing the colleagues with whom they feel comfortable with:

> This method gives students' the responsibility to choose their team colleagues. In this case, it is normal, and it always happens, at least I speak for myself, we are able to work with the colleagues that we know better, are our friends, or that we had worked before, because it is easier because we already know what to expect.

Another advantage they identify is the previous knowledge of the team members. If they know their colleagues, they know what to expect, how to behave and this makes it easier to coordinate the work:

> I prefer working with the colleagues I choose, because I know that I get along well with them, I know how they work, and it is easier to coordinate the task development.

On the other hand, there are also some disadvantages. If the group elements stay together for a long time, some irritation or disagreements can occur, which can lead to poor working environment:

> It will create a bad mood within the group and, in the next tasks, they will feel that the [disagreement] will happen again and the bad mood will continue.

They also identify, as disadvantage, that students may never be selected by their colleagues, either because they are not well known, they arrive late, or they are shy:

> The biggest disadvantage is to continue to isolate the members that were not able to form the groups in the beginning of the semester, by having got late or other reasons.

In these situations, changing the group elements may be beneficial.

2. Teacher-assigned groups

Although there are several possibilities for teacher-assigned groups formation, this theme refers only to randomly assigning students to teams. In the classroom, most of the random assignment was performed with a deck of cards, in which students selected cards randomly and they were put together according to the number of the card they drawn: ace, ones, twos, threes, and so on. This method works well for groups of four elements. With groups of more elements, the suite was used: clubs, spades, hearts and diamonds.

This random assignment appears to be fairer, since contributes to equal opportunities, in the sense that all the students have the same probability to belong to a given team:

> When teachers select the groups, exclusion situations, confusion in the selection process and other problems do not happen.

In addition, they also think that this method of group formation contributes to further develop communication skills, since they have to come forward, overcome the shyness and assume the responsibility to allow the task to be successful:

> Since the group members do not know each other well, they have to overcome the shyness and start communicating, which will help develop the communication skills of everyone with the people that they do not know or that they do not usually relate.

This attitude depends on the social skills of the members. If they cannot overcome the shyness, if they fail to start communicating, the work will suffer and the communication between the members may fail:

> The main disadvantage is the fact of people not feeling comfortable with each other, reducing the communication.

Moreover, the random assignment of members can also lead to unbalanced teams, lacking equity or diversity:

> There can be elements that are lazier in the development of the tasks, or with less individual responsibility, because some think that since the work is to be developed by several students, some will do the work for them. When working in teams, we are participating in a "team game", where we have to succeed. The product of our work will be presented orally or in written, by a representative of the group or by all its elements.

Regardless of the group formation strategy, students also have a rigorous perception of what it represents being a group member and the benefits of working together.

## 3. The learning community

In relation to working in teams, it is possible to identify several categories in the students' text. In addition to the advantages and disadvantages, they also mention the competences developed, and the conditions for the successful development of the task.

Working in teams, regardless of the formation strategy, clearly contributes to equal opportunities, as described in the following excerpt:

> There are more help and support between team mates. If one member has more difficulty with a task, all help, because all want to be successful. It is very stimulating both in the development of the task and in the learning process, always stimulating to do more and better, not for being better than the other members, but to increase the knowledge of all, so that all members win.

On the other hand, the disadvantages lie on the lack of commitment of some elements:

> Impossibility to complete the task because some element forgot essential material that was of his responsibility.

Lack of responsibility and laziness:

> Insufficient individual responsibility and tendency for laziness by some elements.

In addition to the cognitive knowledge developed with the development of the task, students identify the development of communication skills as the most relevant development resulting from team work:

> It [working in teams] really helped me, mainly communicating with the others. I can say that I was a very shy person and I was always afraid of group work.

Of course, group work is only successful if a set of conditions are met. Members should demonstrate flexibility towards the exchange of ideas and integrating the others:

> It can be successful, if there are some flexibility by some team members.

Work is also more successful if the team members have good communication and articulation:

> If the group elements go along well, if they respect each other and the others' opinions, it is easy to work with them [...] the cooperation between the elements, help, shared responsibilities and balanced tasks contributes to successful and pleasant result.

Another condition for successful team work is the previous knowledge of the members abilities. Students constantly refer that if students know each other, the will work better together:

> The fact the students knowing each other, and their work methods is very important, because it contributes to better cohesion and understanding throughout the development of the task.

Finally, responsibility is of paramount importance:

> If the group has members that work but one promises to work but fails the objectives by lack of commitment or by laziness, this leads to the members working alone of by themselves.

Students realize that working in teams is important to their learning process and that prepares them better to work in the modern society. It helps them develop a set of competences that wouldn't exist otherwise. However, successful work depends on some conditions.

4. Change the groups with every new task

    The students' perceptions regarding their participation in groups that change with every task is structured in advantages and disadvantages. The most remarkable advantage is the constant challenge they face when interacting with different colleagues in every task:

    > I have been having a notable development and facing new challenges because I have to learn to adapt and accept working with new people in several tasks.

    Different people are characterized by different knowledge, background, way of working and personality. This enriches the team work with a healthy diversity:

    > Each element has a different personality and his knowledge can be better in an area than in others. The elements complement each other, bringing new perspectives and approaches to each new task.

    Equal opportunities are also identified as an advantage, since:

    > If each task were solved by different teams, students would have to work with everyone else, helping also the closest and the shyest.

    They also refer learning different ways of working, better communication skills and better inter-personal relations:

    > Many times, we have to deal with a group that has to come quickly with creative solutions. I'm always learning new ways to come up with the best solution. Dealing with different people all the time contributes to widen our inter-personal relations.

    Finally, maintaining the groups formation through the semester also has some advantages.

5. Maintain the groups formation through the semester

    The main advantage is the deepening of personal relations:

    > In the groups that are kept unchanged through the semester I managed to create a deeper relation with the other members.

    The disadvantages result from getting too much comfortable, which can lead to tense situations and difficulty in meeting the objectives and the deadlines:

    > Teams that don't change can result in less successful tasks. If the members are too much comfortable, the communication and coordination between them suffers, with members assuming all the work and others relaxing and failing to keep the shared responsibility.

    They also identify less equality, since:

It continues to isolate the students that did not manage to form groups in the beginning of the semester, because they were late or any other reasons.

Regardless of the group formation strategy, the main benefits of group work remain. Students recognize that among some advantages and disadvantages, there are important competences acquired in group work, contributing to equal opportunities. On the other hand, the disadvantages lie on the lack of commitment of some elements, as well as some potential lack of responsibility and laziness (Mesquita & Lopes, 2018).

The perception of the students in relation to several indicators regarding the two possibilities of group formation (groups formed by students and groups formed by the teacher) gives a clear understanding of how they like to work and their perceptions of the team work and about the difficulty to engage in a learning community.

They understand that working with others helps them to learn different ways to work together and they feel that this is important for their development. They also value the exchange of experiences and the respect of the others' opinions.

Looking at the results from the better distribution of the tasks, more effectiveness, it is possible to understand that if they know each other's capacities and skills, work will be more successful. However, these indicators are unbalanced with the less commitment with the tasks and with the higher tendency for a single leader. Students recognize that in student-selected groups, although they are more productive, organized and successful, there is also less commitment and concentrated leadership, which is inconsistent.

The majority of students prefer the comfort of working with whom they know, maintain personal relations of have worked before instead of working with random colleagues.

## 4.3 Collaborative Learning

Assuming the ethical values defined in the framework of this study, the social-constructivism approach was considered, as a pedagogical approach that allows the student to be active in the construction of his knowledge, in the context of an enabling social and emotional environment, built through the interaction and negotiation with the others (Dumont, Istance, Benavides, & OECD, 2010). Classes that assume these principles adopt methodologies that foster collaborative learning, in which students work together, being responsible for their and for the others' learning, learning with technology, in which the latter is an element support the students learning and implement meaningful teaching-learning experiences, formative assessment, as a self-regulated assessment process that allows students to achieve better results, inquiry-based approaches, assumed as relevant to the development of higher-order thinking skills (Lopes, Mesquita, Rio-Rama, & Alvarez-Garcia, 2018).

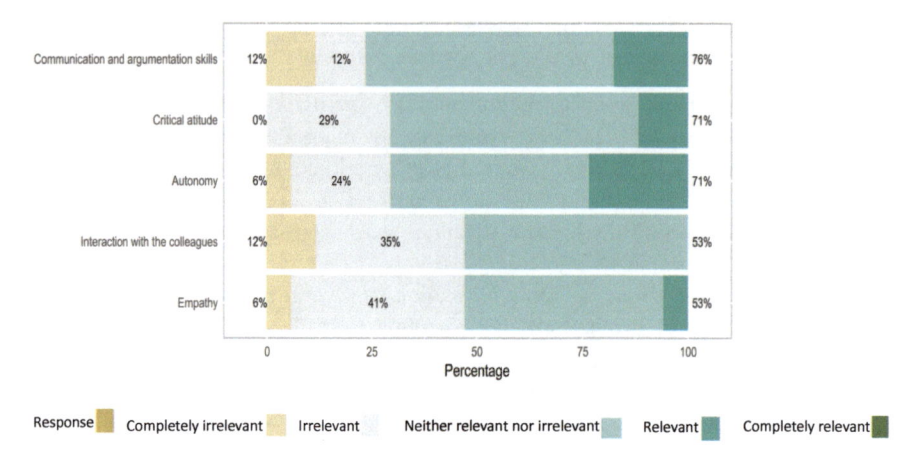

**Fig. 1** Development of ethical skills. Source: Author's own figure

In this context, collaborative learning plays a fundamental role, providing the students with opportunities for developing routines and abilities related to work planning, resource organization, problem solving, delegation, respecting the others opinion and work. Students work together, being responsible for their and for the others' learning. This methodology takes a long time to develop, because students are used to traditional teaching-learning strategies, which appeals to individual action, passive role and little receptive to the others' ideas.

The pedagogical methodologies followed in the two courses mentioned in this chapter, beyond valuing the participation of the student in the dynamics of the learning process, are also designed with their participation and contribution, engaged in enabling environments that stimulates active and experiential learning, with the constant guidance of the teacher (Lopes, 2014; Lopes & Mesquita, 2016).

The development of higher-order thinking skills happens simultaneously with the development of the cognitive skills. Considering the characteristics of the subjects and the degrees, as well as the learning experiences designed within the pedagogical strategies, five skills were considered: communication and argumentation, critical thinking, autonomy, interpersonal relationships and empathy. Each of the skills was sorted according to the importance attributed by the students, from the most important to the least.

Students considered that collaborative learning contributed, in the highest degree, for the development of their communication and argumentation skills, immediately followed by the development of their critical thinking and autonomy (Fig. 1). They valued moderately the work and the interaction with colleagues as well as the empathy, confirming that they believe the work could be more comfortable if more self-centered.

## 5 Conclusions

This study reveals that, to assume an ethical dimension in the classroom, it is necessary that the teaching methodologies change as well as the students' attitudes. It is clear that the development of an enabling learning environment, where the students feel that they participate and effectively contribute to their learning process. However, the introduction of these kind of approaches in a specific moment in the academic path of students is insufficient for the development of a community of learning. The connectedness between subjects and areas will be necessary to reward commitment to quality on teaching and learning processes.

The learning contracts resulted in a facilitating instrument of the development of meaning of belonging, which further allowed each student to situate towards his singularity and to accept the group's diversity.

To provide meaning to a community of learning, implies the development of the feeling of belonging. However, although students consider important to work with all the member of the group, they reveal some bias. Although students prefer the student-selected group formation, they value more the competences and the characteristics that teacher-assigned group formation stimulates in them. Moreover, the challenges that arise from the organizations and from the modern society require that students are prepared to work with different people and to deal with the social diversity. In this sense, it is important, that team work allows them to contact with this cultural, social and intellectual diversity.

Most of the students considered that the learning experiences contributed to the development of community of learning. The role of the teacher is fundamental both for the design of the whole process and for the monitoring and guidance of the students. In this type of strategies, the participation and involvement of students demand a constant and up-to-date feedback. This is one of the aspects that has to be improved, according to the students' opinion.

Education institutions should organize the courses and the methodologies in order to make effective and systematic the participation of students in groups that allows them to work with different colleagues.

The study would benefit from a wider scale implementation, to better assess the implications in more areas and more students. Moreover, it is also beneficial to assess the impact of this process in a longitudinal study, that could reveal the ethical assumptions of students during their professional activity and personal lives.

## References

Chapman, K. J., Meuter, M., Toy, D., & Wright, L. (2006). Can't we pick our own groups? The influence of group selection method on group dynamics and outcomes. *Journal of Management Education, 30*(4), 557–569. https://doi.org/10.1177/1052562905284872.

Dewey, J. (1997). *Democracy and education* (Later Printing ed.). New York: Free Press.

Dumont, H., Istance, D., Benavides, F., & OECD (Eds.). (2010). *The nature of learning: Using research to inspire practice*. Paris: OECD.

Flyvbjerg, B. (2002). Bringing power to planning research: One researcher's praxis story. *Journal of Planning Education and Research, 21*(4), 353–366. https://doi.org/10.1177/0739456X0202100401.

Flyvbjerg, B. (2006). *Making organization research matter: Power, values, and phronesis* (SSRN Scholarly Paper No. ID 2278252). Rochester, NY: Social Science Research Network. Retrieved from https://papers.ssrn.com/abstract=2278252.

Foucault, M. (1980). *Power/knowledge: Selected interviews and other writtings, 1972–1977*. New York: Pantheon Books.

Freire, P. (1970). *Pedagogia do oprimido*. Rio de Janeiro: Paz e Terra.

Gambôa, R. (2004). *Educação, ética e democracia: a reconstrução da modernidade em John Dewey*. Porto: Asa.

Giddens, A. (1986). *The constitution of society: Outline of the theory of structuration* (Reprint ed.). Berkeley: University of California Press.

Gülcan, N. Y. (2015). Discussing the importance of teaching ethics in education. *Procedia – Social and Behavioral Sciences, 174*, 2622–2625. https://doi.org/10.1016/j.sbspro.2015.01.942.

Houssaye, J. (2004). Pedagogia: justiça para uma causa perdida. In J. Houssaye, M. Soëtard, D. Hameline, & M. Fabre (Eds.), *Manifesto a favor dos Pedagogos*. Porto Alegre: Artmed.

Kelly, S., Zavotsky, K. E., Delaney, E., Pagani, C., Duffy, C. P., Haqq-Stevens, E., et al. (2017). Motivation and personal challenges while enrolled in higher education: The pathway to becoming a baccalaureate nurse. *Journal of Nursing Education and Practice, 7*(11), 14. https://doi.org/10.5430/jnep.v7n11p14.

Kemmis, S., & McTaggart, R. (2005). Participatory action research: Communicative action and the public sphere. In N. K. Denzin & Y. S. Lincoln (Eds.), *The Sage handbook of qualitative research* (pp. 559–603). Thousand Oaks, CA: Sage. Retrieved from https://researchonline.jcu.edu.au/26655/.

Knoch, M. (2004). A importância do estudo da ética no ensino superior: uma reflexão epistemológica. *Interações, 7*, 81–99.

Lave, J. (1988). *Cognition in practice*. Cambridge: Cambridge University Press.

Lopes, R. P. (2014). An award system for gamification in higher education. In L. G. Chova, A. L. Martinez, & I. C. Torres (Eds.), *Iceri2014: 7th international conference of education, research and innovation* (pp. 5563–5573). Valenica: IATED. Retrieved from http://apps.webofknowledge.com/InboundService.do?mode=FullRecord&customersID=RID&IsProductCode=Yes&product=WOS&Init=Yes&Func=Frame&DestFail=http%3A%2F%2Fwww.webofknowledge.com&action=retrieve&SrcApp=RID&SrcAuth=RID&SID=C33U4B2D7PZsEcTM4Ia&UT=WOS%3A000367082905091.

Lopes, R. P., & Mesquita, C. (2016). A Gamificação e a IBL na Aprendizagem dos Alunos do Ensino Superior. In *VII Congresso Mundial de Estilos de Aprendizagem: livro de atas* (pp. 1162–1175). Bragança: Instituto Politécnico de Bragança. Retrieved from http://hdl.handle.net/10198/12934.

Lopes, R. P., Mesquita, C., Rio-Rama, M. de la C. del, & Alvarez-Garcia, J. (2018). Collaborative learning experiences for the development of higher-order thinking. *Revista ESPACIOS, 39*(17). Retrieved from http://www.revistaespacios.com/a18v39n17/18391716.html.

MacIntyre, A. C. (2007). *After virtue: A study in moral theory* (3rd ed.). Notre Dame: University of Notre Dame Press.

Magalhães, J. (1999). Um apontamento para a história do manual escolar: entre a produção e a representação. In R. Castro, A. Rodrigues, J. Silva, & M. Sousa (Eds.), *Manuais escolares. Estatuto, funções, história* (pp. 277–301). Braga: Instituto de Educação e Psicologia, Centro de Estudos em Educação e Psicologia.

Maqtary, N., Mohsen, A., & Bechkoum, K. (2017). Group formation techniques in computer-supported collaborative learning: A systematic literature review. *Technology, Knowledge and Learning*. https://doi.org/10.1007/s10758-017-9332-1.

Mesquita, C., & Lopes, R. P. (2018). Assessing students' participation under different group formation strategies. In *EDULEARN18 Proceedings* (pp. 9802–9811). Palma de Maiorca: IATED.

Pijano, C., Scott, P., & Knight, J. (2014). *The state of higher education 2014* (Report). Retrieved from OECD website. Accessed February 16, 2019, from http://www.oecd.org/education/imhe/StateofHigherEducation2014.pdf

Roschelle, J., & Teasley, S. D. (1995). The construction of shared knowledge in collaborative problem solving. In *Computer supported collaborative learning* (pp. 69–97). Berlin: Springer. https://doi.org/10.1007/978-3-642-85098-1_5.

Stump, G. S., Hilpert, J. C., Husman, J., Chung, W., & Kim, W. (2011). Collaborative learning in engineering students: Gender and achievement. *Journal of Engineering Education, 100*(3), 475–497. https://doi.org/10.1002/j.2168-9830.2011.tb00023.x.

Van den Bossche, P., Gijselaers, W. H., Segers, M., & Kirschner, P. A. (2006). Social and cognitive factors driving teamwork in collaborative learning environments: Team learning beliefs and behaviors. *Small Group Research, 37*(5), 490–521. https://doi.org/10.1177/1046496406292938.

Vygotsky, L. S., Cole, M., Cipolla Neto, J., Menna Barreto, L. S., & Afeche, S. C. (2008). *A formação social da mente o desenvolvimento dos processos psicológicos superiores*. São Paulo: Martins Fontes.

Wenger, E. (2010). Communities of practice and social learning systems: The career of a concept. In C. Blackmore (Ed.), *Social learning systems and communities of practice* (pp. 179–198). London: Springer. https://doi.org/10.1007/978-1-84996-133-2_11.

# Geotourism in Latin America and Caribbean UNESCO Global Geoparks: Contribution for Sustainable Development Goals

Emmaline M. Rosado-González, José Luis Palacio-Prieto, and Artur Abreu Sá

**Abstract** A key feature of the UNESCO Global Geoparks (UGGps) is their contribution to regional sustainable development through initiatives and strategies of geoconservation, geoeducation and geotourism, promoted in cooperation with the local communities. In this sense, UGGps are committed to promote and carrying out activities that contribute to Agenda 2030 and its 17 Sustainable Development Goals (SDG). This Agenda, established in 2015 by United Nations, is assumed as a plan for planet, people, peace, prosperity and partnerships.

The geotourism as one of the main axes of the UGGps, sensu Arouca Declaration (2011, aroucageopark.pt/documents/78/Declaration_Arouca_EN.pdf), and the geotouristic initiatives developed on UGGps could be an effective tool to contribute for the sustainable development of these territories.

This work is part of a broader research that aims to characterize the contribution of UGGps in Latin America and Caribbean (LAC) region to the Agenda 2030 and its 17 SDGs. However, in this work we focused mainly on the impacts of geotourism in the UGGps. The main objective is to show some evidences on how the geotourism strategies and activities carried on the four UGGps in LAC until early 2019 (Araripe UGGp in 2006—Brazil; Grutas del Palacio UGGp in 2013—Uruguay, Comarca Minera UGGp and Mixteca Alta UGGp in 2017—Mexico) are contributing in the scope of the SDG 8, SDG 9, SDG 10, SDG 11 and SDG 15.

The field work research was composed on the application of questionnaires and the development of workshops with the local communities of these four territories. The obtained results were based on the perception of the local communities and the

---

E. M. Rosado-González (✉) · A. A. Sá
UNESCO Chair on Geoparks, Sustainable Regional Development and Healthy Lifestyles, University of Trás-os-Montes e Alto Douro, Vila Real, Portugal

Geoscience Centre of University of Coimbra, Coimbra, Portugal

J. L. Palacio-Prieto
Earth Sciences National School and Geography Institute, National Autonomous University of Mexico, Mexico City, Mexico

impression they have of the impacts of the UGGps on their territories. This allowed to describe the evidences on how UGGps contribute on different ways to the Agenda 2030, particularly showing the impact of geotourism in specific targets, such as employment promotion, establishment of sustainable infrastructures, reduction of inequalities and the environmental conservation, among others. This work explains with a concrete case study the benefits that each territory can gain with a good promotion of geotourism strategies under the UGGp label.

**Keywords** UNESCO Global Geoparks · Sustainable Development · Latin America and Caribbean · SDG 8 · SDG 9 · SDG 10 · SDG 11 · SDG 15

## 1 Introduction

During the United Nations Conference on Environment and Development, held in Rio de Janeiro in 1992, was adopted by 178 Governments the Agenda 21, known as the "Rio Declaration on Environment and Development, and the Statement of principles for the Sustainable Management of Forests". This Agenda was assumed as "*a comprehensive plan of action to be taken globally, nationally and locally by organizations of the United Nations System, Governments, and Major Groups in every area in which human impacts on the environment*" (UN, 2018). This initiative still being considered one of the most relevant precursors of the world sustainable development initiatives.

In this scenario the different programs and initiatives worldwide focused on the sustainable development of the territories consider this Agenda as one of their main backgrounds. This is the case of the UNESCO Global Geoparks (UGGps). The Agenda 21 was followed-up by diverse international protocols and agreements focused on the its different topics. As example of this reality we can mention the Istanbul Programme of Action for the Least Developed Countries, the Paris Climate Change Agreement, the Addis Ababa Action Agenda, the Sendai Framework for Disaster Risk Reduction, the Education 2030 Incheon Declaration and Framework for Action, the Strategic Plan for Biodiversity 2011–2020, the Aichi Targets, and the Millennium Development Goals (UN, 2016a; UNESCO, 2015a, 2015b).

In 2000, the United Nations (UN) established the Millennium Development Goals (MDGs) which intended to be a 15 years plan, which ranged from halving extreme poverty rates to halting the spread of HIV/AIDS and providing universal primary education up to 2015 (UN, 2016a, 2016b, 2016c, 2016d). The MDGs then established considered eight main goals:

- Eradicate extreme poverty and hungry;
- Accomplish universal primary education;
- Promote equality gender and woman autonomy;
- Reduce infant mortality;
- Improve maternal health;

- Fight IHV/AIDS, malaria and other diseases;
- Guarantee environmental sustainability;
- Promote a global association for development.

However, after this time frame, the UN decided in 2015 to go forward with this plan, establishing the Agenda 2030 for Sustainable Development, which was assumed as a plan for planet, people, peace, prosperity and partnerships, composed by 17 Sustainable Development Goals and 169 targets.

In this scope, was also in 2015 that the General Assembly of UNESCO approved the creation of the International Geosciences and Geoparks Programme (IGGP), which assumed the compromise to work towards the Agenda 2030. Nowadays there are 147 UGGps around the world in 41 countries. In Latin America and Caribbean (LAC) until now we have seven UGGps: Araripe UGGp, recognized in 2006 in Brazil; Grutas del Palacio UGGp, recognized in 2013 in Uruguay; Comarca Minera UGGp and Mixteca Alta UGGp, both recognized in 2017 in Mexico; Kültralkura UGGp, recognized in 2019 in Chile; Colca y Volcanes de Andagua UGGp, recognized in 2019 in Peru; and Imbabura UGGp, recognized in 2019 in Ecuador.

The UGGps are territories where sites and landscapes of geological relevance are managed trough a holistic way of protection, education and sustainable development involving the local communities (UNESCO, 2019). The UGGps management structure is based in three main axis of action: geoconservation, geoeducation and geotourism. The last one is defined as the tourism which sustains and enhances the identity of a territory, taking into consideration its geology, environment, culture, aesthetics, heritage and the well-being of its residents (Arouca Declaration, 2011). In this sense, the geotourism can be a way to contribute to the United Nations Agenda 2030 for local sustainable development, particularly on the SDG 8 "promote sustained, inclusive and sustainable economic growth, full and productive employment and decent work for all"; the SDG 9 "build resilient infrastructure, promote inclusive and sustainable industrialization and foster innovation"; the SDG 10 "reduce inequality within and among countries"; the SDG 11 "make cities and human settlements inclusive, safe, resilient and sustainable"; and the SDG 15 "protect, restore and promote sustainable use of terrestrial ecosystems, sustainably manage forests, combat desertification, and halt and reverse land degradation and halt biodiversity loss" (UN, 2015).

## 2 UNESCO Global Geoparks and Their Framework in Latin America and Caribbean

In 1996, during the 30th International Geological Congress held in Beijing, at the geological heritage session, was discussed what should be the appropriate strategies to promote geoconservation. The last concept should be interpreted as the conservation of geodiversity due to its intrinsic, ecological and geo-patrimonial values. In the other hand, geodiversity must be interpreted as the range (or diversity) of the geological, geomorphological and soil attributes, as well as their interaction, systems and processes (Sharples, 2002).

In this context, the objectives of a program of conservation and promotion of sites of geological interest began to be developed: *"The idea behind the initiative is that true sustainable territorial development can be achieved through the protection and promotion of geological heritage through scientific, educational and tourism activities"* (Zourous, 2004).

In 1997, during the 29th General Conference of UNESCO held in Paris, the idea of creating a global network of sites of geological relevance was raised for the first time and was referred into the UNESCO's official document 29 C/5, section II.4.2 (02036).

In April 1999, during the 156th session of UNESCO, was formally proposed for the first time the "UNESCO Geoparks Program" as a new initiative to promote a global network of geoparks, with the objective of safeguarding and developing areas selected for their significant geological features. In this meeting stands out some main topics (UNESCO, 1999):

- The Division of Earth Sciences takes the initiative to coordinate and combine the different national and international efforts in favor of geoconservation and the identification of geosites, as well as to prepare the scenario for future activities in geological heritage conservation and the possibility of establishing a geoparks program under the auspices of UNESCO;
- Is recognized the need to highlight and disseminate the value of geological heritage through representative examples under a sustainable local development approach in both developing and developed countries;
- The Geoparks Program will constitute a complementary activity to the International Geological Correlation Program that focuses on Earth science research;
- To promote the preservation and international recognition of geological heritage by the geoparks program it is not covered by another UNESCO program, nor by any other conservation program. The launch of the Geoparks Program will provide excellent means for the international recognition of sites of geological interest. Considering the different objectives of the World Heritage Convention and the Global Network of Biosphere Reserves, the Geoparks Program will constitute a complementary activity for the preservation of the natural and cultural heritage;
- A geopark will be an area dedicated to highlight the geological features that stand out for their meaning, rarity or beauty, and that are representative of the geological history of a particular area;
- A geopark, in addition to the possibilities of conducting scientific research and environmental education, must have a high potential for sustainable local development, must generate jobs and new economic activities linked to the specific theme of the geopark;
- Every geopark that submits its candidacy to UNESCO must present a management structure and management plan in a context of sustainable development.

The conclusions of that meeting included the proposal of the Geoparks Program in document 30 C/5 (UNESCO's program and budget for the biennium 2000–2001), under the existing structures of the UNESCO International Geological Correlation Program. In this document, within the section on the main actions to promote the management of the terrestrial system, consideration was given to the possibility of creating a UNESCO Geoparks Program within the strategies for the year 2000–2001. At the same time, was suggested a feasibility study in the development of a UNESCO Geoparks Program, in order to improve the international recognition of sites with geological interest to promote the conservation of the Earth's heritage (UNESCO, 2000).

In 2000, the European Geoparks Network (EGN) was founded with the participation of four territories with a significant geological heritage: the Geological Reserve of Haute-Provence (France); the Petrified Forest of Lesbos (Greece); Vulkaneifel (Germany); and Cultural Park of Maestrazgo (Spain).

In April 2001, in the Cabo de Gata-Nijar Natural Park (Spain), during the meeting for the "Management of protected natural spaces and sustainable development", the EGN signed a formal validation agreement with the Earth Sciences Division of UNESCO (referred to in document 161 EX/Decisions, 3.3.1), which established the bases of collaboration between the EGN and UNESCO. Nowadays the EGN is formed by 75 Geoparks in 25 countries.

In February 2004, an international group of UNESCO experts, meet in Paris, agreed on the establishment of the Global Geoparks Network, which included at this time 17 European Geoparks and 8 Chinese Geoparks. In June of the same year, during the First International Geoparks Conference held in Beijing (China), the Global Geoparks Network (GGN) under the auspices of UNESCO was formally established. The GGN is an international organization committed to the conservation, management and communication of the Earth's heritage. Today the GGN counts with 147 Geoparks.

More recently, during the 38th General Conference of UNESCO (November 2015), the 195 UNESCO Member States approved unanimously the International Geoscience and Geoparks Programme (IGGP). This ratified the UGGps as the most recent and innovative territories that promotes sustainable development in a holistic perspective, considering education, local development, scientific research, protection and promotion of natural and cultural heritage (UNESCO, 2016a).

Regarding this new reality, UNESCO established the following guidelines that any Geopark should accomplish to become a UGGp (UNESCO, 2016b):

1. Must be single, unified geographical areas where sites and landscapes of international geological significance are managed with a holistic concept of protection, education, research and sustainable development.
2. UGG should use that heritage, in connection with all other aspects of that area's natural and cultural heritage, to promote awareness of key issues facing society in the context of the dynamic planet we all live on.
3. UGG should be areas with a management body having legal existence recognized under national legislation.

4. In the case where an applying area overlaps with another UNESCO designated site, such as a WHS or MAB, the request must be clearly justified, and evidence must be provided for how UGG status will add value by being both independently branded and in synergy with the other designations.
5. UGG should actively involve local communities and indigenous peoples as key stakeholders in the Geopark. In partnership with local communities, a co-management plan needs to be drafted and implemented in accordance with the social and economic needs of local populations, looking forward the protection of the landscape in which they live and conserves their cultural identity.
6. UGG are encouraged to share their experience and advice and to undertake joint projects within the Global Geoparks Network Association (GGNa). Membership of GGNa is obligatory.
7. A UGG must respect local and national laws relating to the protection of geological heritage. The defining geological heritage sites within a UGG must be legally protected in advance of any application.

In the Latin America and Caribbean (LAC) region, the interest on stablish geoparks started in 2004 and Araripe Global Geopark (Ceará, NE Brazil) was the first one to be formalized in this continental area (Herzog, Sales, & Hillmer, 2008; Piranha, Lama, & Bacci, 2011). Other initiatives appeared in several countries of the LAC region such as Argentina, Bolivia, Brazil, Chile, Colombia, Costa Rica, Cuba, Ecuador, Mexico, Nicaragua, Peru, Uruguay and Venezuela. Just in 2013 another territory became part of the GGN: the Grutas del Palacio in Uruguay (Pereira, 2013). After this, in 2017, two more territories became part of the UGGps, the Comarca Minera UGGp and the Mixteca Alta UGGp, both in Mexico (Palacio, Rosado-González, & Miranda, 2018). In April 2019 were formalized by UNESCO three new UGGps in LAC: Kültralkua (Chile), Colca y Volcanes de Andagua (Peru) and Imbabura (Ecuador). Despite this, the reality is that more than 50 projects aspiring to be nominated as UGGps in the short and middle-term.

Since 2008, several meetings were carried out in order to consolidate a regional network to promote the establishment of new territories in LAC. The first significant outcome of these meetings were the Araripe Declaration, signed in 2010 in Brazil. This was followed by the Melipeuco Declaration, signed in 2011 in Chile, and the Arequipa Declaration, signed in 2015 in Peru. In these documents was established on one hand the need of promote the creation of more Geoparks in LAC region, on the other hand, was declared the relevance and particularities of the indigenous cultures that are relevant. In order to achieve this goals and territorial sustainability, was also declared the importance of the networking and joint efforts among the UGGps and aspiring territories (Araripe Declaration, 2010; Arequipa Declaration, 2015; Melipeuco Declaration, 2015).

As of 2015, the territories in LAC start a more consistent work in order to consolidate the UGGps and develop new aspiring projects. This implied the application of three new projects from Mexico (Comarca Minera and Mixteca Alta) and Ecuador (Tungurahua). The UNESCO outcome was the approval of the two Mexican territories (May 2017) and a 2 years deferred of the Ecuadorian territory. In 2016 the territory Colca y Volcanes de Andagua (Peru) applied to become a UGGp but was also deferred. In 2017 five more aspiring projects from LAC applied to UNESCO to became UGGps: Kütralkura (Chile), Imbabura (Ecuador), Chirripo (Costa Rica), Tacaná Volcano (Mexico) and Rio Coco (Nicaragua). The two first ones together with Colca y Volcanes de Andagua (Peru) were approved as UGGps in April 2019.

In 2017, the four UGGps then existing in the region created the Latin America and Caribbean UNESCO Global Geoparks Network (GeoLAC) during the 4th Latin America and Caribbean Symposium of Geoparks in Arequipa (Peru) (Palacio et al., 2018).

Recently, the UNESCO Chair on "Geoparks, Sustainable Regional Development and Healthy Lifestyles", held in the University of Trás-os-Montes e Alto Douro (Portugal), promoted the initiative to create an Observatory for Sustainable Development in the Latin America and Caribbean UGGps. This initiative, currently under construction, aims to be a forum and a platform for divulgation, discussion and networking for experiences and good practices to be shared among the UGGps and aspiring territories in LAC, towards the development of geoconservation, geoeducation and geotourism strategies for sustainability.

## 3 United Nations Agenda 2030 for Sustainable Development and Geotourism

Between 2005 and 2014, under the scope of the Millennium Development Goals, the UN General Assembly declared a "Decade of Education for Sustainable Development (DESD)" with the main goal to create public awareness for the importance of sustainable development taking into account the education plans (UNESCO, 2016c). The DESD emerged with the argument that education is an indispensable element for achieving sustainable development. In this context, the main goal of the DESD was to integrate in all aspects and ways of education, the principles and values of sustainable development through coordinated efforts of several UN agencies, programmes and organizations (UN, 2016a; UNESCO, 2016d).

At the end of the DESD 10 conclusions emerged: (1) Education systems are addressing sustainability issues; (2) Sustainable development agendas and education agendas are converging; (3) Political leadership has proven instrumental; (4) Multi-stakeholder partnerships are particularly effective; (5) Local commitments are growing; (6) Whole-institution approaches help practice ESD; (7) ESD facilitates interactive, learner-driven pedagogies; (8) ESD is being integrated into formal education; (9) Non-formal and informal ESD is increasing; (10) Technical and vocational education and training advances sustainable development (UNESCO, 2014). In this framework, DESD evolves into the Global Action Programme (GAP) on Education for Sustainable Development. This Programme aimed to be the follow-up of the DESD efforts and contribute to the ESD initiatives of the 2030

Agenda (UNESCO, 2016e). The overarching goal of the GAP is "*to generate and scale up action in all levels and areas of education and learning to accelerate progress towards sustainable development*". To achieve this aim, the GAP established as main objectives: (1) to reorient education and learning so that everyone has the opportunity to acquire the knowledge, skills, values and attitudes that empower them to contribute to sustainable development; (2) to strengthen education and learning in all agendas, programmes and activities that promote sustainable development (UNESCO, 2016e).

In continuity, in 2015 was approved the Agenda 2030 for Sustainable Development, which comprises 17 main objectives with 169 goals focused on establishing better life quality for everyone trough adequate practices of development, taking into account the social, economic and environmental sectors. In this sense, the Agenda 2030 emerged like a continuation of the MDGs, mainly focused on sustainable development, especially in the least developed countries (UN, 2016a).

This was the main reason for the implementation of the Agenda 2030, in order to continue the task of the MDGs making an emphasis in the economic, social, and environmental dimensions of sustainable development (UN, 2015, 2016a).

In this context, the Agenda 2030 establishes the following 17 Sustainable Development Goals:

SDG1—End poverty in all its forms everywhere;
SDG2—End hunger, achieve food security and improve nutrition and promote sustainable agriculture;
SDG3—Ensure healthy lives and promote well-being for all at all ages;
SDG4—Ensure inclusive and equality quality education and promote lifelong learning opportunities for all;
SDG5—Achieve gender equality and empower all women and girls;
SDG6—Ensure availability and sustainable management of water and sanitation for all;
SDG7—Ensure access to affordable, reliable, sustainable and modern energy for all;
SDG8—Promote sustained, inclusive and sustainable economic growth, full and productive employment and decent work for all;
SDG9—Build resilient infrastructure, promote inclusive and sustainable industrialization and foster innovation;
SDG10—Reduce inequality within and among countries;
SDG11—Make cities and human settlements inclusive, safe, resilient and sustainable;
SDG12—Ensure sustainable consumption and production patterns;
SDG13—Take urgent action to combat climate change and its impacts;
SDG14—Conserve and sustainably use the oceans, seas and marine resources for sustainable development;
SDG15—Protect, restore and promote sustainable use of terrestrial ecosystems, sustainably manage forest, combat desertification, and halt reverse land degradation and halt biodiversity loss;

SDG16—Promote peaceful and inclusive societies for sustainable development, provide access to justice for all and build effective, accountable and inclusive institutions at all levels;

SDG17—Strengthen the means of implementation and revitalize the Global Partnership for Sustainable Development.

These 17 goals emerged from three principal attention axes: end poverty, fight inequalities and injustice, tackle climate change; and recognize five important action sectors (5Ps): the people, the planet, the prosperity, the peace and the partnerships (UN, 2015).

The Agenda 2030 also take into account different programmes and initiatives which seek improvements in education, environment, health and wellbeing like the Istanbul Programme of Action for the Least Developed Countries (IPoA), Paris Climate Change Agreement (PA), Addis Ababa Action Agenda (AA), Sendai Framework for Disaster Risk Reduction (SF), Education 2030 Incheon Declaration and Framework for Action (ID), Strategic Plan for Biodiversity 2011–2020 and the Aichi Targets (SPB) (UNESCO, 2015a, 2015b).

The Istanbul Programme of Action for the Least Developed Countries established particular strategies for the special needs of the least developed countries in order to achieve the MDGs and now the SDGs for the 2011–2020 decade; IPoA identify eight priority areas of action: (1) Productive capacity; (2) Agriculture, food security and rural development; (3) Trade; (4) Commodities; (5) Human and social development; (6) Multiple crises and other emerging challenges; (7) Mobilizing financial resources for development and capacity building; (8) Good governance at all levels (UNESCO, 2015b).

The Paris Climate Change Agreement is an international agreement between 193 United Nations Member States to strength efforts to combat climate change trough national commitments focused on reduce global carbon emissions (UN, 2016c).

The Addis Ababa Action Agenda is an agenda of more than 100 concrete measures to enhance global partnership in order to finance practices and investments in sustainable development good practices trough technology, science, innovation, trade and capacity building. This agreement was reached by 193 UN Member States (UN, 2016d).

The Sendai Framework for Disaster Risk Reduction is a 15-year voluntary agreement adopted by UN Member States to reduce disaster risk through partnerships between local governments, private sector and other stakeholders. The SF establish Four Priorities for Action: (1) Understanding disaster risk; (2) Strengthening disaster risk governance to manage disaster risk; (3) Investing in disaster risk reduction for resilience; (4) Enhancing disaster preparedness for effective response and to "Build Back Better" in recovery, rehabilitation and reconstruction (UNISDR, 2016).

The Education 2030 Incheon Declaration and Framework for Action overarching goal is to continue the efforts done to reach the second MDG "Accomplish universal primary education" and contribute to reach the fourth SDG "Ensure inclusive and equitable quality education and promote lifelong learning opportunities for all" (UNESCO, 2016f).

The Strategic Plan for Biodiversity 2011–2020 and the Aichi Targets it is a 10-year plan of actions between Member States to safeguard biodiversity and continued the efforts on awareness the value of biodiversity and their environmental services (CBD, 2016).

In this entire framework, the geotourism, as one of the main axes of the management structure of UGGps, could implement strategies that can contribute to the Agenda 2030, particularly in the SDGs 8, 9, 10, 11 and 15. The geotourism as one of the tourism segments, appeared in the 1990s decade and was originally defined as a educative sustainable tourism on geological sites, mainly quarries and mines, promoting the access trough interpretative trails that allows to conserve these sites (Hose, 1996).

Afterwards, the concept evolved in different ways, until was formally presented and discussed, among GGN, ProGEO and the National Geographic's Center for Sustainable Destinations of National Geographic Society, in 2011 in the Arouca UGGp during the International Congress of Geotourism. In this meeting were stablished that the geotourism is: *"tourism which sustains and enhances the identity of a territory, taking into consideration its geology, environment, culture, aesthetics, heritage and the well-being of its residents. Geological tourism is one of the multiple components of geotourism"* (Arouca Declaration, 2011). In this sense, the geotourism promotion in the UGGps can be a tool for the contribution on strategies for the sustainable development.

## 4 Methodology Proceedings

This work is part of a broader research, currently under development, which aims to characterize the contribution of LAC UGGps for the Agenda 2030 and its 17 ODS. However, this work intends to be focused on the impact of geotourism in the economy, employment, infrastructure development, reduction of inequalities, the creation of sustainable social dynamics, and environmental conservation aspects in four LAC UGGps, in which the main aim is to carry out a specific analysis of the contribution of these territories for SDGs 8, 9, 10, 11 and 15.

In this context, the first step was to identify which of the SDGs targets were more compatible with the objectives of the UGGps. After the selection of the targets (Table 1), indicators were postulated for a survey that was applied to inhabitants of the four territories.

For the SDG 8 were selected seven of the 12 targets; for the SDG 9 were selected five of the eight targets; for the SDG 10 were selected four of the 10 targets; for the SDG 11 were selected five of the 10 targets; and for the SDG 15 were selected three of the 12 targets defined by United Nations (UN, 2015).

The target population of this work resulted from a selection of persons with greater proximity to the UGGps, such as coordination team members, tourism

**Table 1** Targets selected for each SDG

|  | Targets selected |
|---|---|
| SDG 8 | 8.1, 8.2, 8.3, 8.5, 8.6, 8.8, 8.9 |
| SDG 9 | 9.1, 9.2, 9.4, 9.5, 9.c |
| SDG 10 | 10.2, 10.3, 10.4, 10.7 |
| SDG 11 | 11.2, 11.3, 11.4, 11.7, 11.c |
| SDG 15 | 15.1, 15.2, 15.3 |

Source: Author's own table

service providers, school principals and teachers, representatives of local companies, artisans, farmers, guides-interpreters, museum and interpretation center managers, among others.

The application of this methodology in each of the LAC UGGps provided information about the inhabitants' perception of how UGGps are contributing to the SDGs, as well as identifying where there is lack of impact. This reality also allowed to identify potential strategies for its implementation in the UGGps, in order to achieve sustainable development according to the needs of the local population.

## 5 Results

During the fieldwork, a total of 367 surveys were applied, of which 94 were in the Araripe UGGp, 86 in the Grutas del Palacio UGGp, 95 in the Comarca Minera UGGp and 92 in the Mixteca Alta UGGp. The results obtained for the UGGps contribution to the 17 SDGs showed that SDGs 5, 10, 11 and 17 are those that have a greater impact on the territories.

On the other hand, regarding the contribution of the LAC UGGps for SDGs 8, 9, 10, 11 and 15, was noticeable that of the four territories studied, Araripe UGGp and Grutas del Palacio UGGp were those that reported more benefits, and the Comarca Minera UGGp was the one that reported the least benefits.

Concerning the contribution of the LAC UGGps for the SDG 8, the Grutas del Palacio UGGp was the territory with more impact, and Comarca Minera UGGp is the one with less impact. About the specific targets of the SDG 8, the four UGGps in LAC demonstrates higher contribution for the target 8.9. Secondly and thirdly targets with more contribution are the 8.1 and 8.2. The target 8.8 was the one with less contribution by the four UGGps. As example of a contribution for this goal can be mentioned the creation of a "geoproduct" label in Grutas del Palacio UGGp. This is a quality certification ascribed to local and sustainable products that aims to help the economic growth through an innovative strategy of promotion of the native culture and products.

Regarding the SDG 9, the Araripe UGGp was the territory with more contribution evidences, followed by Grutas del Palacio UGGp, Mixteca Alta UGGp, and Comarca Minera UGGp. About the specific targets of this goal, was founded out that the target 9.1 was the one with more influence, followed by the targets 9.2, 9.4 and 9.c, respectively (Fig. 1). As example on how the UGGps are contributing to this

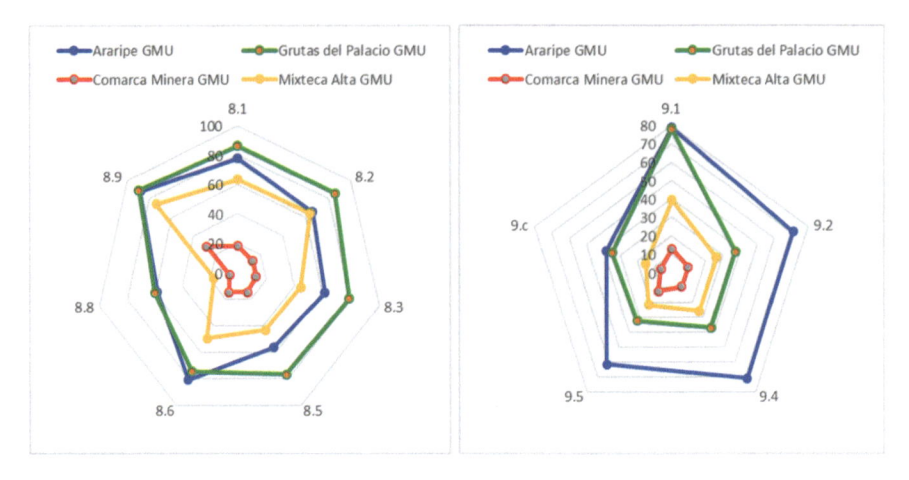

**Fig. 1** Contribution of the four LAC UGGps to the targets chosen from SDG 8. Source: Author's own figure

SDG, the Comarca Minera UGGp created a research laboratory in an old mine, mainly focused on dark matter observation. This laboratory in addition to geophysics research, promotes geotourism through educational activities for science disclosure and allows to visit the geological and cultural heritage linked to the old mine where the laboratory is built. This also promotes scientific research in the region and increase the number of researcher workers.

Concerning SDG 10, Grutas del Palacio UGGp and Araripe UGGp were the territories with more contribution, followed by Mixteca Alta UGGp and Comarca Minera UGGp, respectively. Regarding the contribution in the specific aims, the targets 10.2 and 10.3 were those with highest contribution by the UGGps, followed by the targets 10.4 and 10.7, respectively. In the Araripe UGGp it was possible to find good examples of how the UGGps contribute to the SDG 10 through geotourism. The management structure developed a trail for the disability people—trail of the senses—where disabled persons can experience a trail in full contact with the nature, involving and including them as the most important visitors of this specific area. The Araripe UGGp also contributes to SDG 10 trough different *fora* of discussion and experience sharing with focal groups such as women, artisans, guides and children, among others, in order to support them on their involvement and participation within the community, helping to create a healthier social environment.

Regarding the SDG 11, the Grutas del Palacio UGGp and Araripe UGGp were the ones with more impact, followed by Mixteca Alta UGGp and the Comarca Minera UGGp, respectively. Concerning the impact for the specific targets, the 11.4 was the most relevant in the four territories, followed by the targets 11.7, 11.3, and 11.2, respectively (Fig. 2). In this context, the four LAC UGGps studied have good examples of contribution. Due their initiatives of geotourism they aim to safeguard and conserve the natural and cultural heritage of their territory's trough the promotion of environmental educative activities.

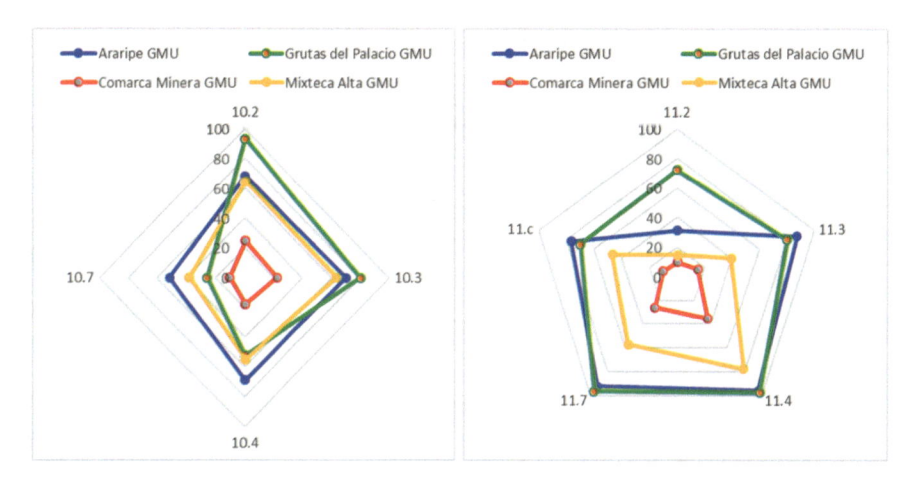

**Fig. 2** Contribution of the four LAC UGGps to the targets chosen from SDG 10. Source: Author's own figure

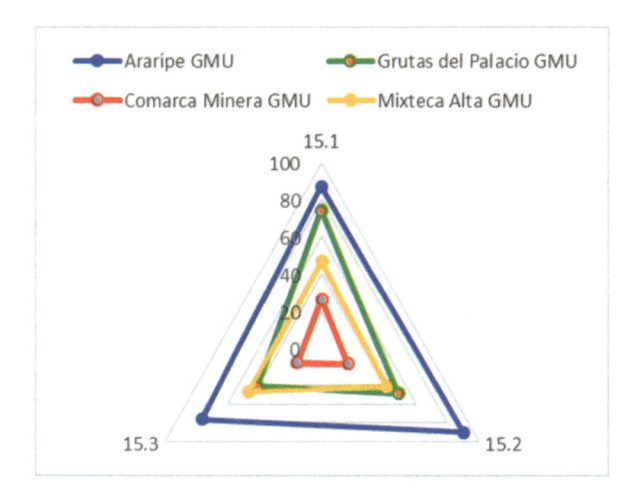

**Fig. 3** Contribution of the four LAC UGGps to the targets chosen from SDG 15. Source: Author's own figure

Concerning to the SDG 15, the Araripe UGGp was the territory with highest contribution, followed by Grutas del Palacio UGGp, Mixteca Alta UGGp, and Comarca Minera UGGp, respectively (Fig. 3). The target for which these territories most contribute is the 15.1, followed by 15.2 and 15.3, respectively. One example on how the LAC UGGps contributes to SDG 15, is the case of Mixteca Alta UGGp, where some geotourism activities they had implement, in an innovative strategy to involve the visitors in the communality activities, are related with reforestation, conservation, cleaning of green and natural areas, among others, that aims to restore and protect the environment of the area.

## 6 Discussion and Conclusions

The results processed allowed to discriminate differences and similarities between the four UGGps territories studied. One noteworthy aspect is the evidence the most recent UGGps had less impact on the contribution to SDGs than older ones. Regarding this, it should be noted that the Araripe UGGp reveals a consistent path in this issue, already demonstrating a strong participation of the local community and being possible to observe evident benefits. In contrast, the Comarca Minera UGGp reveals a lower impact and contribution to the SDGs, which demonstrate the efforts to engage and to empower the community for Agenda 2030 sustainable development goals are still at an early stage.

Each UGGps have a management structure, based on different and specific territorial approaches. In the case of the Araripe UGGp and Mixteca Alta UGGp, their management bodies are based on the university's researchers, students and technical teams. On the other hand, the Grutas del Palacio UGGp and Comarca Minera UGGp management structures are based on regional governments. This difference has impacts on the way the UGGps are impacting in the territories and dealing with the implementation of sustainable development practices.

In this sense, the way on how they implement geotourism strategies have different approaches, some of them focused on educational activities, others focused on the community involvement, but all of them with the common goal of contribute decisively for sustainable development.

## References

Araripe Declaration. (2010). *First Latin America and the Caribbean Conference of Geoparks*. Ceará. Accessed March 6, 2017, from http://geoparkararipe.org.br/wp-content/uploads/2015/08/Araripe-Declaration.pdf

Arequipa Declaration. (2015). *First symposium on Geoparks, geological heritage and geotourism*. Arequipa. Accessed March, 8, 2017, from http://geoparkararipe.org.br/wp-content/uploads/2015/08/Declaraci%C3%B3n-de-Arequipa-1.pdf

Arouca Declaration. (2011). Accessed April 1, 2019, from aroucageopark.pt/documents/78/Declaration_Arouca_EN.pdf

CBD. (2016). *Strategic plan for biodiversity*. Accessed November 16, 2016, from https://www.cbd.int/undb/media/factsheets/undb-factsheet-sp-en.pdf

Herzog, A., Sales, A., & Hillmer, G. (2008). *The UNESCO Araripe Geopark: A short story of the evolution of life, rocks and continents*. Governo do Estado de Ceará, p. 71.

Hose, T. (1996). Geotourism, or can tourists become casual rock hounds? In M. R. Bennett (Ed.), *Geology on your doorstep* (pp. 207–228). London: The Geological Society.

Melipeuco Declaration. (2015). Accessed April 2019, from http://geachile.sernageomin.cl/en/useful-documents/16-declaracion-melipeuco.html

Palacio, J., Rosado-González, E., & Miranda, G. (2018). *Geoparques: Guía para la formulación de proyectos*. Geografía para el Siglo XXI, Instituto de Geografía, UNAM, p. 224.

Pereira, R. (2013). *El Sistema Nacional de Áreas Protegidas de Uruguay, avances y perspectivas*. Tesis de Diplomado en Gestión de Áreas Naturales. Universidad de la República Uruguay, p. 45.

Piranha, J., Lama, E., & Bacci, D. (2011). Geoparks in Brazil—Strategy of geoconservation and development. *Geoheritage, 3*, 289–298.

Sharples, C. (2002). *Concepts and principles of geoconservation*. Publishes electronically on the Tasmanian Parks and Wildlife Service. http://www.dpiw.tas.gov.au/inter.nsf/Attachments/SJON-57W3YM/$FILE/geoconservation.pdf

UN. (2015). *Transforming our world: The 2030 Agenda for sustainable development*. Accessed March 15, 2019, from https://sustainabledevelopment.un.org/content/documents/21252030%20Agenda%20for%20Sustainable%20Development%20web.pdf

UN. (2016a). *Millennium development goals*. Accessed October, 15, 2016, from http://www.un.org/millenniumgoals/

UN. (2016b). *Decade of education for sustainable development*. Accessed November 14, 2016, from http://www.desd.org/about.html

UN. (2016c). *Paris climate change agreement*. Accessed November 15, 2016, from http://unfccc.int/paris_agreement/items/9485.php

UN. (2016d). *Financing for development*. Addis Ababa Agenda. Accessed November 16, 2016, from http://www.un.org/esa/ffd/ffd3/press-release/countries-reach-historic-agreement.html

UN. (2018). *Agenda 21*. Accessed March, 25, 2019, from https://sustainabledevelopment.un.org/index.php?page=view&nr=23&type=400&menu=35

UNESCO. (1999, April 15). *UNESCO Geoparks Programme—A new initiative to promote a Global Network of Geoparks safeguarding and developing selected areas having significant geological features*. Executive Board, Hundred and fifty-sixth Session, 156 EX/11 Rev.

UNESCO. (2000). *Proyecto de Programa y Presupuesto 2000–2001*, 30 C/5, Conferencia General 30° reunión.

UNESCO. (2014). *Shaping the future we want: UN decade of education for sustainable development (2005–2014)*. Final Report, 201 pp.

UNESCO. (2015a). *MAB strategy 2015–2025*. Accessed November 14, 2016, from http://www.unesco.org/new/fileadmin/MULTIMEDIA/HQ/SC/pdf/MAB_Strategy_2015-2025_final_text.pdf

UNESCO. (2015b). *Sustainable development in the least develop countries. Towards 2030.* Accessed October 20, 2016, from http://unesdoc.unesco.org/images/0024/002448/244835E.pdf

UNESCO. (2016a). *UNESCO Global Geoparks*. Accessed October 15, 2016, from http://unesdoc.unesco.org/images/0024/002436/243650e.pdf

UNESCO (2016b) *Statutes of the International Geoscience and Geoparks Programme*. Accessed October 15, 2016, from http://www.unesco.org/new/fileadmin/MULTIMEDIA/HQ/SC/pdf/IGGP_UGG_Statutes_Guidelines_EN.pdf

UNESCO. (2016c). *UN decade of education for sustainable development*. Accessed October 2016, from http://unesdoc.unesco.org/images/0014/001416/141629e.pdf

UNESCO. (2016d). *UN decade of ESD*. Accessed November 15, 2016, from http://en.unesco.org/themes/education-sustainable-development/what-is-esd/un-decade-of-esd

UNESCO. (2016e). *Global action programme*. Accessed November 15, 2016, from http://en.unesco.org/gap/goals-and-objectives

UNESCO. (2016f). *Education 2030 Incheon declaration and framework for action*. Accessed November 16, 2016, from http://www.uis.unesco.org/Education/Documents/incheon-framework-for-action-en.pdf

UNESCO. (2019). *UNESCO Global Geoparks*. Accessed April 1, 2019, from http://www.unesco.org/new/en/natural-sciences/environment/earth-sciences/unesco-global-geoparks/

UNISDR. (2016). *Sendai framework for disaster risk reduction*. Accessed November 16, 2016, from http://www.unisdr.org/we/coordinate/sendai-framework

Zourous, N. (2004). The European Geoparks Network; Geological heritage protection and local development. *Episodes, 27*(3), 165–171.

# Social Innovation in Refugee Support: Investigating Prerequisites Towards a Conceptual Framework

**Phyllis McNally, Nikolaos Apostolopoulos, and Haya Al-Dajani**

**Abstract** This paper investigates the required elements in the advancement of social innovation (SI) produced by entrepreneurial organisations. These efforts are to assist the establishment of a new conceptual framework including the voices of those, most vulnerable and ferociously impacted by not only local but also global crisis. Qualitative data by an organisation which educates social workers and refugees fuel the concept of social innovation by pointing to the interplay of structure and agency as well as social issues and impact on economy. Our existing knowledge on the role of social enterprises and refugee support through social innovative services are limited. Social innovation is closely linked to social entrepreneurship (SE) in practice and in literature. SE in context of refugee support is a concept currently gaining attention. Social innovation could be equally relevant in this regard. SI is a broad, versatile term, believed to hold a yet fully to be discovered potential. While SI is not a new revelation it is, however contested as a term and is yet to be fully understood, defined and diffused for it to be exploited at its maximum potential.

**Keywords** Innovation · Social enterprise · Social innovation · Refugees

---

A major portion of this chapter has been taken from the Masters thesis of Phyllis McNally submitted successfully for the award of MSc Business and Management by University of Plymouth, UK

P. McNally (✉) · N. Apostolopoulos · H. Al-Dajani
Plymouth University, Plymouth, UK
e-mail: phyllis.mcnally@postgrad.plymouth.ac.uk; Nikolaos.apostolopoulos@plymouth.ac.uk; Haya.al-dajani@plymouth.ac.uk

© Springer Nature Switzerland AG 2020
V. Ratten (ed.), *Technological Progress, Inequality and Entrepreneurship*, Studies on Entrepreneurship, Structural Change and Industrial Dynamics,
https://doi.org/10.1007/978-3-030-26245-7_8

## 1 Introduction

Mulgan (2006) stresses the growing diversity of countries and cities demand social innovative ways of organising schooling, language learning, housing and conflict management. This becomes more important in the case of social innovative ways of supporting refugees. In the first 9 months of 2015, 487,000 people seeking refuge entered Europe, doubling the number from the whole of 2014 (Banulescu-Bogdan & Fratzke, 2015: in Holmes & Castaneda, 2016). According to Holmes and Castaneda (2016) there are estimates of over one million more refugees yet to come, leading the European Commission to call this the 'largest global humanitarian crisis' of our time (Holmes & Castaneda, 2016). The Young Foundation (2012) explain impeding the interception of these challenges are silos in the public sector, market failures in the private sector and a lack of scale and fragmentation in the civil sector. SI could be the answer to overcoming these challenges. Where these overarching challenges and failures impact on some of the most vulnerable individuals such as refugees, SI must be investigated in this context to enable potential solutions while deepening an understanding of the SI concept.

While efforts are made to advance SI in the academic arenas and SI is occurring in practice settings they happen often unknowingly (Stott & Tracey, 2018). Mulgan (2006) criticises that the absence of sustained and systematic analysis is holding back the practice of SI, making it harder to detect gaps in current provision of funding, advice, and support. To this extent, this paper aims to contribute to our existing knowledge by investigating the missing elements in the progress of social innovation, especially when targeting vulnerable groups such as refugees through social enterprising. With that said, the recent trends in literature regarding achieving the Sustainable Development Goals through entrepreneurial activities highlight the importance of social entrepreneurship and social innovation (Apostolopoulos, Al-Dajani, Holt, Jones, & Newbery, 2018).

The paper is structured across five chapters. After the introductory chapter, the second chapter critically reviews literature revolving around social innovation. The third chapter introduces the case study organisation, followed by the research design including findings, discussion and lastly concluding remarks.

## 2 Theoretical Background

Social innovation is a disputed term which has been defined often generically as the creation and implementation of new solutions to social problems, holding benefits that are shared beyond the confines of the innovators (Elsen, 2014; Matei & Antonie, 2015; Tracey & Stott, 2016). Significant work is still required to identify a comprehensive SI definition (Ayob, Teasdale, & Fagan, 2016; Cajaiba-Santana, 2014; De Bruin & Read, 2018; Kocziszky & Somosi, 2016; Lorenz & Elsen, 2014; Matei & Antonie, 2015; Mulgan, Tucker, Ali, & Sanders, 2007; Nicholls, Simon, & Gabriel,

2015; The Young Foundation, 2012; Tracey & Stott, 2016; Van der Have & Rubalcaba, 2016; van Niekerk et al., 2017). Bulut, Eren, and Halac (2013) claim the SI concept can develop original and sustainable ideas to problems that range in a spectrum from working conditions to education, individual or societal development, tracking health and environment as well as climate change. Elsen (2014) raises the definition to more complex explanation and goes on to combine the functions of social innovations which act within levels of society such as the micro (e.g. changes in family structures), the meso (such as new institutional arrangements) or the macro (e.g. Social Security for everyone), with these levels existing in structures (such as flatter hierarchies), processes (e.g. participative planning) and individual agency of the innovative thinkers allowing the spark of innovation to ignite and come to realisation. Lisetchia and Brancu (2013) explain:

> Various definitions approach the social innovation concept by observing different aspects: what is social innovation, which is the object of the innovation process, which are its motives and effects, which is the object of change, which is the targeted area of change, which are the components (Lisetchia & Brancu, 2013, p. 89).

Edwards-Schachter, Matti, and Alcántara (2012) investigated 76 journals to examine social innovation definitions on characteristics associated with SI and the correlating dimensions; Aims, Purposes/objectives, Drivers, Sources, Context, Agents, Sectors, Process, Empowerment and capacity building (social capital), Governance, Results/outcomes. SI principal approaches and structural intersections interplay between the individualist, organisational and regional/national approach (Unceta, Castro-Spila, & García Fronti, 2016).

Considering Elsen's (2014) SI definition above of the micro, meso and macro levels, the complexity of social innovation processes becomes fully apparent in Unceta et al. (2016) analysis of approaches for SI indicators. However, the drivers to innovate are diverse but certainly include: necessity, responding to unmet needs, sharing a vision of what can be, achieving legitimacy in the eyes of external power and resource brokers (Stott & Tracey, 2018, p. 1).

Community-based social purpose organisational forms, predating social enterprise are often overlooked by innovation researchers, but Stott and Tracey (2018) place great relevance on these. They claim the concept innovation is traceable way back to over a century ago (Stott & Tracey, 2018). Despite rapidly growing SI literature which may offer the illusion SI is brand new, its history has been traced back at least as far as to the beginnings of cooperatives (Bobic, 2013; Stott & Tracey, 2018). In 1844, the Rochdale Pioneers brought to life the cooperatives to answer social problems of the time, that still prevail today (The Rochdale Principles—Rochdale Pioneers Museum, 2017). The Co-operative is now an international movement and applies a bottom-up approach giving equal power to all participants (Bobic, 2013).

Numerous social innovations created by community or civil society actors (Nicholls & Murdock, 2012; van Niekerk et al., 2017) evidence SI embodies a bottom-up approach and relies on the fundamental understanding that communities and citizens can interpret their own lives, recognise problems and competently find solutions (Mulgan et al., 2007).

Despite SI's wide application the concept holds considerable gaps in research. Mulgan (2015) believes SI research lacks evidence of value creation and destruction of social innovation, in as so far that it follows the same principle of innovation with its creation of value for some, but destruction of value for others. This research gap can be drawn back to Schumpeter (1942: In Carter & Jones-Evans, 2012) and his view of economic development, being a process of creative destruction with entrepreneurs playing a key role in the introduction and expansion of some enterprises whilst other enterprises simultaneously exit or collapse. However, this is not a phenomenon that occurred as abruptly as perceived but rather a continuous process of citizens wanting their needs heard and support (Carter & Jones-Evans, 2012). Kocziszky and Somosi (2016) believe innovation plays a key role in the constancy for the performance of an economy and see a correlation between the innovation potential of a region and its ability to produce economic output. Economists have long known SI functions as a compensating factor for a lack of economy and science innovation (Kocziszky & Somosi, 2016). Moreover, the European Union in the past decades pay great attention to the context of SI linked to social changes, incorporating it into their objectives for the programming period of 2014–2020 (Kocziszky & Somosi, 2016).

## *2.1 Social Entrepreneurship and Social Innovation*

Social entrepreneurs are called on by Dees (1998, 2001) to develop new models for a new century. It is expected social enterprises to be the vehicle of social innovation (The Young Foundation, 2012) which is in line with the European Commission (2017a) vested interests in entrepreneurship. There has been a developed understanding of the importance of innovation for the future of European competitiveness and the global economy reflected in the European Commission (2017b) statement:

> The EU is implementing policies and programmes that support the development of innovation to increase investment in research and development, and to better convert research into improved goods, services, or processes for the market (European Commission, 2017b: online).

Al-Dajani, Carter, Shaw, and Marlow (2015) examined entrepreneurship aimed for social purposes in their research on destitute women who accessed micro-loans to improve their living standards. A focus on the value of entrepreneurship as a strategy for economic and social development is debated and whether entrepreneurship aimed at eliminating poverty and aiding marginalised peoples, in fact, can be an instrument of improvement or involuntarily cause disempowerment (Al-Dajani et al., 2015). Social entrepreneurship could be perceived as a swift, simple fix to aid stabilising economies whilst freeing those, most in need, from poverty. Data collated by Al-Dajani et al. (2015) suggest 'entrepreneuring' was pursued by research participants as a means available to 'get by' rather than an opportunity to 'break free'. Nonetheless, the means of entrepreneurship were proven to fulfil a social function here insofar as support for disadvantaged women was offered with the scheme to provide microloans encouraging enterprise, enabling an income to be generated.

Dees (1998, 2001) claims SE did not have to rely solely on not-for-profit structures but takes advantage of social purpose for-profit business structures or hybrid organisations with a combination of not-for-profit and for-profit elements. Social entrepreneurs are entrepreneurs with a social mission and face challenges due to their socially orientated mission (Dees, 1998, 2001). Progression in social entrepreneurship research increasingly focus on similar efforts in relation to refugees and SE (Betts, Omata, & Bloom, 2017; Bizri, 2017; Chahine & Grom, 2017; Marchand & Dijkhuizen, 2018; Obschonka & Hahn, 2018). Stott and Tracey (2018) take a critical stance to social entrepreneurship and the process of creating and growing a venture to address social challenges, which they believe is swiftly becoming the 'go to' strategy for policy makers and those aiming to create social change. While current policy, practitioner, and academic literature reiterates social enterprise is an effective response to social ills, Stott and Tracey (2018) warn:

> ...the weight of expectations placed on social entrepreneurship to overcome others' 'failures' is at best unhelpful and at worst counterproductive, not least because sustaining social enterprises appears to be inherently difficult (Stott & Tracey, 2018, p. 6).

Beyond social entrepreneurship, SI is conceptualized as a new avenue to create positive social impact (Van der Have & Rubalcaba, 2016) and it is believed to accelerate in the next hundred years (Mulgan, 2006). The Young Foundation (2012) highlight the issues for global societies are the 'failure' of the modern welfare state, the failure of conventional market capitalism, resource scarcity and climate change, an ageing population and the associated care and health costs, the impact of globalisation, the impact of mass urbanisation and more. Throughout literature SI has been rooted in innovation (Bulut et al., 2013; Lorenz & Elsen, 2014; Matei & Antonie, 2015). Studies conducted by the European Commission show companies prioritising innovation achieve the highest increase in turnover with 79% of companies introducing at least one innovation since 2011 experiencing an increase of their turnover by more than 25% by 2014 (European Commission, 2017c). The initial Innobarometer was a survey collating data on activities and attitudes related to innovation and each year it gathered opinions and feedback from the general public and EU businesses (European Commission, 2017c). The progression of the Innobarometer, in 2016, began to capture details of the main behaviours and trends in innovation-related activities in EU businesses (European Commission, 2017c).

The main results of the research found further action must be taken to support efforts to promote innovation in Europe (European Commission, 2017c). Mulgan et al. (2007) suggest that SI is ever more important for economic growth due to climate change issues or ageing populations which may only be overcome through SI. These crises aren't recent phenomena but rather the interconnection in the context of global systems is elevating these issues to new levels of urgency (Westley, 2008). Tommasi (2015) raises attention to the aftermath of the European Financial Crisis resulting in an ever more pressing need for SI and highlights that the impact of globalisation has become more relevant with the outbreak of the global financial crisis. Globalisation advanced significantly the vast development of civil society and international non-governmental organisations (NGO's) estimated to amount to over 55,000 (Lawrence & Weber, 2017). Key growth sectors in the twenty-first-century are predicted to revolve around health education and care, accounting for around 20–30% of GDP (Mulgan et al., 2007). This change is rooted in the decline of manufacturing and the increasing dominance of service industries (Mulgan, 2006). It is not coincidental that the EU Commission incorporated specific policies on development of social innovation in Horizon 2020 (Elsen, 2014). The re-occurring dialogue on Small to Medium Enterprise's (SME), including NGO's are linked to economy, sustainable future and social innovation. The term SME is often concerned with companies, but the term covers charities, universities, statutory bodies, government and more (GOV.UK, 2017). Westley (2008) argues SI can be aided by market demand or equally by political demand, but these dynamics are as complex as they are difficult to manipulate directly. Charities and NGO's face decreasing funding sources (BBC, 2012; Butler, 2017; May, 2016; Pati, 2011; Tyler, 2016) which is drawing interest in seeking new opportunities and creative ideas to support those most vulnerable. Where NGO's do obtain funding, they may have a better chance to succeed, but such alignment with national and regional funding can violate the organisation's own goals cultural strategies (Dym & Hutson, 2005).

Kestenbaum (2008) claims innovation is crucial to improve public services, ensure economic competitiveness and social wellbeing. Storey and Salaman (2004) believe charities and NGO's are often seen as innovative by their very nature, due to their focus to fulfil unmet social needs. However, not all charitable organisations are truly innovative as they may begin with a new idea, but then settle swiftly into a secure and predictable routine (Storey & Salaman, 2004). Vast amounts of Third Sector organisations explicitly aim to solve or relieve social needs, especially those of disempowered peoples, which makes them important actors in the production of SI (de Wit et al., 2017). Stott and Tracey (2018) argue the survival of people in poor places served by SI depend on it. This is illustrated by the fact that community or civil society actors are the creators of a sizeable number of social innovations (Nicholls & Murdock, 2012; van Niekerk et al., 2017). Howaldt (2018) explains during the last century systematic innovation politics advanced the potential of natural and engineering sciences' research and development and calls for the same pioneer's attitude in the twenty-first century for the quest to advance social practices.

Taking into consideration the current literature, this paper aims to expand our existing knowledge by:

1. Investigating how a social enterprising organisation, which offers services to refugees, develops social innovative initiatives
2. Exploring how social innovation can be further developed by embracing elements that support society to deal with human crisis.

## 2.2 Background of the Case Study Organisation

Informed by the literature review a charity undertaking social entrepreneurial activities was chosen as a case study. Students and Refugees Together (START) has operated in Plymouth, in the South-West of England, since 2001. START has proven to create an innovative learning environment, whilst providing high quality support services to refugees and providing community activities (Butler, 2005, 2017) with social entrepreneurial aspects. While START is part funded by charitable grants, student fees and other smaller income, it also wins large government tenders (START, 2016), supplying significant services as well as contributing to the economy pulling financial resources into the city. Amongst the many START ventures, is the Cultural Kitchen, where upon entry a small contribution or donation is expected by all attendees to part finance a two-course meal and community activities by the charity. START's empowerment ethos and the applied strengths approach (Butler, 2005; Saleebey, 2006) are also vital interest points in exploring the relevance of the bottom-up approach within SI.

# 3 Research Design

This study was undertaken using a social constructivist approach (Young & Colin, 2004: in Andrews, 2012) and triangulation through interviews, focus group and literature review (Chang, 2016) which promoted validity in analysing the research question from multiple perspectives (Brewer & Hunter, 2006; Denzin, 2006). Close, personal ties to START with one of this study's researchers allowed an in-depth, privileged access to a naturally guarded and protected organisation working with vulnerable people. Autoethnographic observations additionally informed findings, ensured authenticity (Diagle, 2015) and heighten relational ethics (Ellis, 2007: in Ellis, Adams, & Bochner, 2011). Through autoethnography a researcher not only aims to make personal experience meaningful and cultural experience engaging, but also reach out wider to a more diverse audience (Bochner, 1997; Ellis, 1995; Goodall, 2006; Hooks, 1994: in Ellis et al., 2011).

Participants for interviews were invited via a circulated email by a START trustee. Students and service users were invited by a staff member to join the focus group. All potential participants were offered a research brief regarding this study digitally or in hard copy and several introductions of the researcher were made to staff, students and service users particularly before or during autoethnographic observations. This sampling approach successfully engaged one trustee and one manager to take part in two in depth interviews as well as a staff member, two placement students and two service users, who are also START volunteers, took part in a focus group. START's founder took on an advisory role in the study and offered significant insights through regular meetings from the outset of the research. Six autoethnographic observations took place in different START settings, two hours per session, with observations and reflections separately recorded afterwards.

## 3.1 Data Collection

Insights from collected data emerged, and relevant themes surfaced throughout the thematic analysis (Braun & Clarke, 2006) of secondary data. These were further expanded by the thematic interview protocols. This in turn was used to guide the focus group session. START's founding trustee contributed essential insights in an advisory capacity throughout all research phases with regular meetings at Plymouth University. Detailed minutes were taken. The interviews were framed around an overarching understanding of START as an organisation and its impact on service users, students and the city in which it is located. The focus group centred on participant experiences and perceptions of support services in Plymouth.

Interviews lasted approximately 1 h. One interview took place at Plymouth University, the other interview and the focus group took place at START. With permission, interviews and the focus group were recorded for transcription under assurances of anonymity and confidentiality. Pseudonyms were used to protect identities. Debriefs after interviews and the focus group added further insights. The constructivist approach (Ponterotto, 2005) combined with interviews, focus group and observations were appropriate for the exploratory nature of this study (Barcik 2017; Saunders, Lewis, & Thornhill, 2016). These methodological decisions acknowledge the extent to cultural and linguistic barriers to conduct research in an organisation with significant diversity, to gather insight ethically and appropriately.

## 3.2 Data Analysis

Analysis of the evidence commenced simultaneously with data collection which provided the opportunity and flexibility to probe potentially interesting issues as they emerged. This ensured, whilst focused on substantive research interests, data collection also incorporated participant perceptions, experiences and voices. An inductive approach was pursued in the analytical process (Corbin & Strauss, 2008). Critical themes and related categories were refined, developed and removed throughout the empirical data reduction process. Corbin and Strauss (2008) believe regardless of research project size it is paramount to integrate as many perspectives as is feasible to ensure depth, insight and richness of data obtained. Through pre-existing relationships to START we were privileged to share the confidences of participants, engaging extraordinarily vulnerable individuals and capturing their contributions to this research. Data were organised in tables to support the process of comparison of emerging themes and categories. These were compared with the additional data collected and knowledge acquired from the secondary research data. NVivo word frequency queries were run and assisted in the initial coding: Meetings with minutes taken with the founding trustee were not included in the word search as they were not recorded or transcribed. Comparisons and coding in a cyclical process (Miles, Huberman, & Saldana, 2014), allowed the progressing from open nodes, confirming

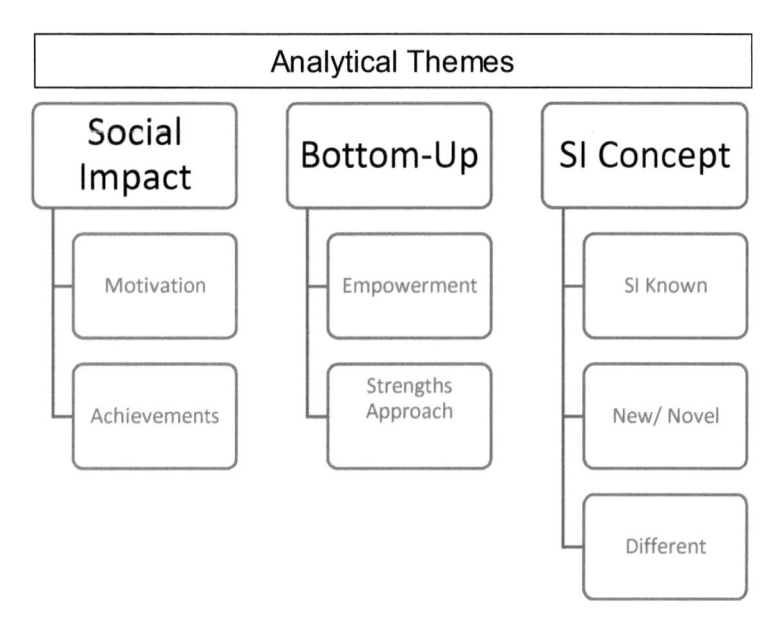

```
                    Analytical Themes
    ┌──────────────┬──────────────┬──────────────┐
    Social          Bottom-Up      SI Concept
    Impact
    │               │              │
    ├─ Motivation   ├─ Empowerment ├─ SI Known
    │               │              │
    └─ Achievements └─ Strengths   ├─ New/ Novel
                      Approach     │
                                   └─ Different
```

**Fig. 1** Analytical themes

the established analytical themes, through to axial codes (Corbin & Strauss, 2008), identifying categories and relationships between categories as seen in Fig. 1.

The literature review established noteworthy lines of inquiry which developed in tandem with empirical data. The analytical themes, their respective categories and examples of raw data are presented in Table 1.

## 3.3 Findings

Van der Have and Rubalcaba (2016) conceptualise SI as a new avenue to create positive social impact. Social impact and its subcategories motivation and achievements bring together an understanding this vital aspect of SI at START. START's intentions to shape a better society clearly articulated by a trustee (Table 1) echoes in the achievements the manager speaks on in terms of students who are impacted by their placements and carry this into their professions impacting on their practice in the community. Further the manager states in relation to service users accessing START support *'that huge movement in people's lives is a huge achievement'*. Aiding those in crisis to rebuild their lives and contribute positively to their communities is tremendous success, but also to highly prepare professionals and thereby a wide-reaching impact is achieved.

Under the bottom up theme empowerment and the strength perspective are categories which resonate with SI's bottom-up approach as understood by Mulgan et al. (2007), Nicholls and Murdock (2012) and van Niekerk et al., (2017). Service

**Table 1** Analytical themes, categories and examples of raw data

| Themes | Categories | Examples of raw data |
|---|---|---|
| Social impact | Motivation | 'It's like our work is to do something that is better, to make something better a better society for us to live in....'(trustee) <br> 'because my work is not about refugees (laughs) it's about possibility, it's about human possibility' (trustee) |
| | Achievements | 'I think the impact student placements had on them becoming professionals out there working the field.' (manager) |
| | | 'Just look at the number of people who've worked with us. Just that huge movement in people's lives is a huge achievement. And I'm not saying people wouldn't have achieved that without START, but I think having START there has really enabled people to move through a very difficult system ....' (manager) |
| Bottom up | Empowerment | 'It is important to empower people, to support them the right way.' (student 1) |
| | | 'You know if you're trying to help trying to create for themselves, trying to do things for themselves then the community is growing.' (service user 1) |
| | Strength's approach | 'So, there's a focus on empowerment on the service users, it's very strength focused. they focus on the strength of the service user, but also the students as well.' (service user 1) |
| | | 'It's really, the service users telling their stories and us taking that on in how we support them so it's really a partnership. (student 1) |
| SI concept | SI known | 'We have a panel where we sit to bring up an idea called conversation club which is a club to explain or to involve refugees that don't really have basic English .... So, this is the basic, like a foundation... it's an innovation actually.' (service user 1) |
| | New/novel | '...looking at innovation is something being new, is innovative. Everything we do we try and look at new models of practice, um, new ways of doing. We are really open to that. (manager) |
| | | 'I think innovation is something new. So, it is starting something that has a ...that comes from and impacts on social relationships.' (trustee) |
| | | 'They (students) help them (refugees) to settle down and they learn more about where they're coming from which is something new and then they bring the information into the office and into the council and into other organisations. '(service user 1) |
| | Different | 'This placement is different in a cultural way. In my previous placement I was dealing with people who are mainly Caucasian. It will bring up the opportunities how to communicate with different organisations and how to communicate with people from diverse ethnic background.' (student 1) |
| | | 'Different students come each year. People come with different ideas.' (manager) |

User 1 believes empowering individuals enables them in '...*trying to do things for themselves*...' and she concludes consequently'...*then the community is growing.*' And links to the social impact sought from social innovation. This is further underlined by Service User 1 highlighting '...*focus on the strength of the service user, but also the student...*' demonstrating the required equality reinforced at

START. This is the fertile foundation allowing vital contributions made from all individuals involved in this support service processes.

Through word search the SI concept theme the three most prominent words associated to SI were established. Wording such as 'new or 'novel' which also can be found in various SI definitions in literature, did not appear to a significant extent in interviews or the focus group other than definitions of SI offered by trustee and manager (Table 1). The word 'different' came up 76 times during interviews and the focus group. The lack of social innovation in the word frequency searches evidences word search limitations. Social innovation by and large was found to be an unknown entity amongst all participants in this study, therefore no direct requests were made for participants to offer a definition of SI.

From the raw data examples interlinked with relevant literature informed findings resulting in response to this paper set out goals.

1. Investigating how a social enterprising organisation, which offers services to refugees, develops social innovative initiatives

    '....it's about human possibility' (Trustee, Table 1) is the quote found in the data which best describes START. The fundaments and ethos of the organisation creates the basis in which possibilities are fostered and people are nourished.

    Hence, the most remarkable finding in this research is the contribution by Service User 1, a refugee woman who is a START service user and volunteer. Service User 1 confidently voiced her understanding of SI and how it translated in activities at START such as the Conversation Club created by service users. Service User 1 states in this context '... *this is the basic, like a foundation... it's an innovation actually.*' The conversation club is a social innovation with social impact and a bottom-up orientation. Based on this we believe a greater focus ought to be redirected in SI literature in the consideration of who the stakeholders in SI are and what they may or may not contribute in the progression of a new SI framework for social initiatives supporting refugees. It was not possible to fully establish who exactly are all stakeholder's in social innovation and where or how it can be determined to involve these in reframing SI within refugee support. However, the initial steps evidencing the importance in pursuing this line of inquiry to develop a new framework for SI has been set. Had data only been considered from the literature review in conjunction with trustees and management input, very different conclusions would have been drawn. The privileged access possible in obtaining data gave new insights from vulnerable individuals rightfully protected by organisations assisting them.

2. Exploring how social innovation can be further developed by embracing elements that support the society to deal with human crisis.

    At the crossovers of academic research, professional practice and the maximising of stakeholder engagement is the potential to fully understand and determine social innovation and all it holds within. Only when both research and practice increase the engagement of informants to SI development is the concept likely to develop fully. Figure 2 emphasises the importance of stakeholders in SI to enrich both the academic and practice-led understanding of SI.

**Fig. 2** Stakeholder involvement (Source: Phyllis McNally, 2018)

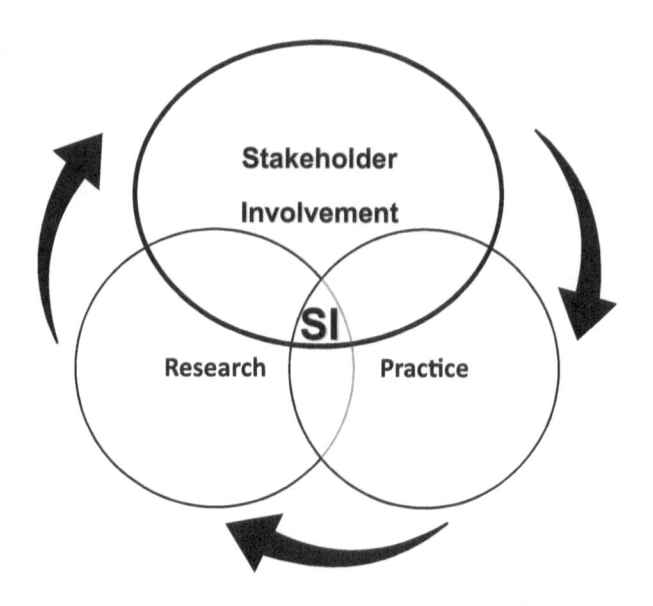

Through understanding who SI stakeholders are and how they best contribute to advancing SI, there is a possibility for bridges to be built between academia and professional practice informed by those who currently have a quiet voice, if a voice at all.

## 4 Discussion

The strengths approach applied at START highlights the importance of every individual being the expert of their own lives (Saleebey, 2006) and during the interview the START trustee speaks of the considered effort of instilling this approach throughout START. Relating the qualities of applying the strengths approach to SI, Mulgan (2006) states:

> Some of the most effective methods for cultivating social innovation start from the presumption that people are competent interpreters of their own lives and competent solvers of their own problems. (Mulgan, 2006, p. 6)

This study involved service users, students, staff and leadership allocating equal relevance to all input gathered, ensuring a bottom-up approach instilled within the research design. The most impactful contribution was made by Service User 1, a young woman who swiftly developed an understanding of SI through the focus group discussions and articulated confidently how and where SI takes place. This highlights the importance and the effectiveness of expanding the stakeholder pool exponentially to inform social innovation in order that those impacted the most by it contribute and guide its interpretation, comprehension and application.

This paper investigated literature around social innovation, recognising it as a contested term whilst considering the concepts positioning within SME's, the economy and the role it plays within local and global crisis. Findings from the empirical data demonstrate within the process of enquiry vital knowledge on SI. Young Foundation (2012) urge that reaching a common understanding of the term is critical if the field is to mature and develop further. Murray, Caulier-Grice, and Mulgan (2010) argue that the design of services should start from the user, and that its diffusion should be approached from the perspective of users, not least because they are in many cases also co-producers. The promotion of SI has focused on the supply side and how innovations can be diffused among service providers through experts, intermediaries, and collaboration (Murray et al., 2010). Dym and Hutson (2005) believe community-based organisations align themselves with their communities because if they didn't then services may be refused and lead to the organisation failing. Therefore, leadership that aligns with community and other group cultures increases the organisation's chance of success (Dym & Hutson, 2005). Lorenz and Elsen (2014) echo Mulgan's prediction of service industries being the biggest growth areas in the economy and take this further in claiming the process must be coming from the bottom up. This is poignant in terms of where input is sought in SI processes and how this informs understanding and diffusion of social innovation.

## 5 Concluding Remarks

Recognising social innovations essential role where social impact is needed whether in economic changes, welfare shifts, or global crisis highlights the imperative in advancing SI. In this regard, understanding who is impacted by SI leads to identifying voices who will contribute crucial perspectives.

Wording is a relevant aspect to consider in future research, particularly where diverse participants are involved, and the meaning of social innovation may need to be improved through offering more information to research participants. This, however, may increase the risk of influencing responses to research questions.

As with any study, we recognise limitations but suggest these offer scope for future research. This study began with a collation of varied SI definitions and the conclusion was reached given the constraints of space, we only consider in a lesser detail the theoretical issues raised by diverse definitions and reserve the endeavour to collect larger volumes of SI definitions for research with more suitable lines of enquiry in this respect. For reasons of confidentiality we were not able to include sections of data from the focus group. Restrictions in this projects scale allowed merely a brief survey on SI case studies as well as limiting the investigation into other SME's such as START to a very basic understanding. However, a larger sample would offer more emerged themes in future research.

Undeniably, SI can offer clarity in strategy, new solutions, improved services, extended comprehension of stakeholder involvement, novel approaches in building equality and a fairer, more sustainable world. Therefore, research and practice efforts to further the concept, fully define and diffuse it will continually prosper.

# References

Al-Dajani, H., Carter, S., Shaw, E., & Marlow, S. (2015). Entrepreneurship among the displaced and dispossessed: Exploring the limits of emancipatory Entrepreneuring. *British Journal of Management, 26*(4), 713–730. https://doi.org/10.1111/1467-8551.12119.

Andrews, T. (2012). What is social constructionism? *Grounded Theory Review, 11*(1), 39–46. Groundedtheoryreview.com [online]. Accessed September 8, 2017, from http://groundedtheoryreview.com/2012/06/01/what-is-social-constructionism/

Apostolopoulos, N., Al-Dajani, H., Holt, D., Jones, P., & Newbery, R. (2018). Entrepreneurship and the sustainable development goals. In D. Crowther & S. Seifi (Eds.), *Entrepreneurship and the sustainable development goals* (pp. 1–7). Bingley: Emerald Publishing Limited.

Ayob, N., Teasdale, S., & Fagan, K. (2016). How social innovation 'came to be': Tracing the evolution of a contested concept. *Journal of Social Policy, 45*(4), 635–653.

Barcik, R. (2017). *5.3 Unstructured, semi-structured and structured interviews* [online]. Accessed June 28, 2017, from https://www.youtube.com/watch?v=gzwGEBJGz8s

BBC. (2012). Charity jobs go as budgets shrink. *BBC News*. Accessed September 16, 2017, from http://www.bbc.co.uk/news/uk-18245690

Betts, A., Omata, N., & Bloom, L. (2017). Thrive or survive: Explaining variation in economic outcomes for refugees. *Journal on Migration and Human Security, 5*, 716.

Bizri, R. M. (2017). Refugee-entrepreneurship: A social capital perspective. *Entrepreneurship and Regional Development, 29*(9–10), 847–868.

Bobic, A. (2013). Co-operatives must become innovation leaders—Co-operative News. *Co-operative News*. Accessed June 28, 2017, from https://www.thenews.coop/40188/sector/retail/co-operatives-must-become-innovation-leaders

Braun, V., & Clarke, V. (2006). Using thematic analysis in psychology. *Qualitative Research in Psychology, 3*(2), 77–101.

Brewer, J., & Hunter, A. (2006). *Foundations of multimethod research*. Thousand Oaks, CA: Sage.

Bulut, C., Eren, H., & Halac, D. (2013). Social innovation and psychometric analysis. *Procedia—Social and Behavioral Sciences, 82*, 122–130.

Butler, A. (2005). A strengths approach to building futures: UK students and refugees together. *Community Development Journal, 40*(2), 147–157.

Butler, P. (2017) Two-thirds of charities subsidising public sector contracts to survive. *The Guardian*. Accessed September 16, 2017, from https://www.theguardian.com/society/2017/may/19/two-thirds-charities-subsidising-public-sector-contracts-survive

Cajaiba-Santana, G. (2014). Social innovation: Moving the field forward: A conceptual framework. *Technological Forecasting and Social Change, 82*, 42–51.

Carter, S., & Jones-Evans, D. (2012). *Enterprise and small business* (3rd ed.). Harlow: Pearson.

Chahine, T., & Grom, E. (2017). *Applying social enterprise to refugee settings (SSIR)* [online]. Ssir.org. Accessed September 28, 2018, from https://ssir.org/articles/entry/applying_social_enterprise_to_refugee_settings#

Chang, H. (2016). *Autoethnography as method*. London: Routledge.

Corbin, J., & Strauss, A. (2008). *Basics of qualitative research: Techniques and procedures for developing grounded theory* (3rd ed.). Thousand Oaks, CA: Sage.

De Bruin, A., & Read, C. (2018). Towards understanding social innovation in multicultural societies: Implications of Māori cultural values for social innovation in New Zealand. *Social Enterprise Journal, 14*(2), 194–207. https://doi.org/10.1108/SEJ-09-2017-0048.

de Wit, H., Gacel-Avila, J., Jones, E., & Jooste, N. (Eds.). (2017). *The globalization of internationalization: Emerging voices and perspectives*. Routledge: Taylor & Francis.

Dees, J. (1998, 2001). *The meaning of "social entrepreneurship"* [online]. Accessed September 10, 2017, from http://e145.stanford.edu/upload/articles/dees_SE.pdf

Denzin, N. (2006). *Sociological methods: A sourcebook* (5th ed.). New Brunswick, NJ: Aldine Transaction.

Diagle, B. (2015) *Making the case for autoethnography* [online]. Accessed August 26, 2017, from https://www.youtube.com/watch?v=gQ1H_2qkpuk

Dym, B., & Hutson, H. (2005). *Leadership in nonprofit organizations*. Thousand Oaks, CA: Sage.

Edwards-Schachter, M. E., Matti, C. E., & Alcántara, E. (2012). Fostering quality of life through social innovation: A living lab methodology study case. *Review of Policy Research, 29*(6), 672–692.

Ellis, C., Adams, T. E., & Bochner, A. P. (2011). Autoethnography: An overview. *Historical Social Research/Historische Sozialforschung, 36*(4), 273–290.

Elsen, S. (2014). Soziale innovation, ökosoziale Ökonomien und community development. In W. Lorenz & S. Elsen (Eds.), *Social innovation, participation and the development of society*. Bozen: Bozen University Press.

European Commission. (2017a). *Promoting entrepreneurship—Growth* [online]. Accessed May 15, 2017, from http://ec.europa.eu/growth/smes/promoting-entrepreneurship_en

European Commission. (2017b). *Innovation—Growth* [online]. Accessed September 10, 2017, from http://ec.europa.eu/growth/industry/innovation_en

European Commission. (2017c). *Innobarometer—Growth* [online]. https://ec.europa.eu/growth/industry/innovation/facts-figures/innobarometer_en

GOV.UK. (2017). *CIRD91200—Corporate intangibles research and development manual—HMRC internal manual—GOV.UK* [online]. Gov.uk. Accessed January 17, 2018, from https://www.gov.uk/hmrc-internal-manuals/corporate-intangibles-research-and-development-manual/cird91200

Holmes, S. M., & Castaneda, H. (2016). Representing the "European refugee crisis" in Germany and beyond: Deservingness and difference, life and death. *American Ethnologist, 43*(1), 12–24.

Howaldt, J. (2018). *Soziale Innovation—Sozialforschungsstelle—TU Dortmund* [online]. Sfs.tu-dortmund.de. Accessed October 8, 2018, from http://www.sfs.tu-dortmund.de/cms/de/Soziale_Innovation/index.html

Kestenbaum, J. (2008). Foreword, In: Woodcraft, S.B., Bacon, N., Faizullah, N. & Mulgan, G., 2008. Transformers: How local areas innovate to address changing social needs.

Kocziszky, G., & Somosi, M. (2016). Generating social innovation with knowledge engineering. *Procedia—Social and Behavioural Sciences, 223*, 167–174.

Lawrence, A., & Weber, J. (2017). *Business and society* (15th ed.). NY: Mcgraw-Hill Education.

Lisetchia, M., & Brancu, L. (2013). The entrepreneurship concept as a subject of social innovation. *Procedia—Social and Behavioural Sciences, 124*(2014), 87–92.

Lorenz, W., & Elsen, S. (2014). *Social innovation, participation and the development of society*. Bozen: Bozen University Press.

Marchand, K., & Dijkhuizen, J. (2018). Entrepreneurship as a tool for a new beginning—Entrepreneurship training for refugees in a new homeland. In *Entrepreneurship and the sustainable development goals* (pp. 135–149). Emerald Publishing Limited.

Matei, A., & Antonie, C. (2015). Complexity theory and the development of the social innovation. *Procedia-Social and Behavioral Sciences, 185*, 61–66.

May, M. (2016). Smaller charities hardest hit by funding cuts since 2008|UK Fundraising. *UK Fundraising* [online]. Accessed September 16, 2017, from https://fundraising.co.uk/2016/02/11/smaller-charities-hardest-hit-by-funding-cuts-research-shows/

McNally, P. (2018). *Development of a qualitative research framework to define social innovation*. Plymouth: Master Thesis, University of Plymouth.

Miles, M., Huberman, A., & Saldana, J. (2014). *Qualitative data analysis*. Thousand Oaks, Calif: Sage.

Mulgan, G. (2006). The process of social innovation. *Innovations, 1*(2), 145–162. Chicago. In Mulgan, G., Tucker, S., Ali, R., & Sanders, B. (2007). Social innovation: What it is, why it matters and how it can be accelerated [online]. Accessed June 28, 2017, from http://eureka.sbs.ox.ac.uk/761/1/Social_Innovation.pdf

Mulgan, G. (2015). Foreword: The study of social innovation—Theory, practice and progress. In A. Nicholls, J. Simon, & M. Gabriel (Eds.), *New frontiers in social innovation research*. UK: Palgrave Macmillan.

Mulgan, G., Tucker, S., Ali, R., & Sanders, B. (2007). *Social innovation*. London: Young Foundation.

Murray, R., Caulier-Grice, J., & Mulgan, G. (2010). *The open book of social innovation*. London: National Endowment for Science, Technology and the Art.

Nicholls, A., & Murdock, A. (2012). The nature of social innovation. In *Social innovation* (pp. 1–30). Vancouver: Palgrave Macmillan.

Nicholls, A., Simon, J., & Gabriel, M. (2015). *New frontiers in social innovation research* [online]. Accessed June 26, 2017, from http://www.transitsocialinnovation.eu

Obschonka, M., & Hahn, E. (2018). Personal agency in newly arrived refugees: The role of personality, entrepreneurial cognitions and intentions, and career adaptability. *Journal of Vocational Behavior, 105*, 173–184.

Pati, A. (2011). Applications soar, but the pot is shrinking. *The Guardian*. Accessed September 16, 2017, from https://www.theguardian.com/voluntary-sector-network/2011/mar/30/foundations-shrinking-pot-grants

Ponterotto, J. (2005). Qualitative research in counseling psychology: A primer on research paradigms and philosophy of science. *Journal of Counseling Psychology, 52*(2), 126–136.

Saleebey, D. (2006). *The strengths perspective in social work practice* (1st ed.). Boston, MA: Pearson/Allyn & Bacon.

Saunders, M., Lewis, P., & Thornhill, A. (2016). *Research methods for business students* (7th ed.). Harlow: Pearson Education.

START. (2016). *Annual report START—Students and refugees together 2015–2016*. Plymouth [online]. Accessed September 4, 2017, from http://www.studentsandrefugeestogether.com/

Storey, J., & Salaman, G. (2004). *Managers of innovation*. Malden, MA: Blackwell.

Stott, N., & Tracey, P. (2018). Organizing and innovating in poor places. *Innovations, 20*(1), 1–17. https://doi.org/10.1080/14479338.2017.1358093.

The Rochdale Principles—Rochdale Pioneers Museum. (2017). *Rochdalepioneersmuseum.coop* [online]. Accessed June 29, 2017, from http://www.rochdalepioneersmuseum.coop/about-us/the-rochdale-principles/

The Young Foundation. (2012). *Social innovation overview: A deliverable of the project: "The theoretical, empirical and policy foundations for building social innovation in Europe" (TEPSIE), European Commission—7th framework programme*. Brussels: European Commission, DG Research.

Tommasi, D. (2015). Social innovation in times of crisis. *Innovation: The European Journal of Social Science Research, 28*(4), 423–424. https://doi.org/10.1080/13511610.2015.1108039.

Tracey, P., & Stott, N. (2016). Social innovation: A window on alternative ways of organizing and innovating. *Innovation: Organization and Management, 19*(1), 51–60. https://doi.org/10.1080/14479338.2016.1268924.

Tyler, D. (2016). In four years there will be no grants for charities—It will destroy communities. *The Guardian* [online]. Accessed September 16, 2017, from https://www.theguardian.com/voluntary-sector-network/2016/feb/11/grants-local-charities-campaign-appeal-government-cuts

Unceta, A., Castro-Spila, J., & García Fronti, J. (2016). Social innovation indicators. *Innovation: The European Journal of Social Science Research, 29*(2), 192–204. https://doi.org/10.1080/13511610.2015.1127137.

van der Have, R. P., & Rubalcaba, L. (2016). Social innovation research: An emerging area of innovation studies? *Research Policy, 45*(9), 1923–1935.

van Niekerk, L., Chater, R., Naydenova, E., Lim, J., Chamas, L., Manderson, L., et al. (2017). *Social innovation in health: Case studies and lessons learned from low- and middle-income countries*. Geneva: World Health Organization. Licence: CC BY-NCSA 3.0 IGO.

Westley, F. (2008). *The social innovation dynamic, social innovation generation*. University of Waterloo [online]. Accessed January 16, 2018, from http://sig.uwaterloo.ca/research-publications